Mindset

Unlocking the Power of Positive Thinking: Skyrocketing your Confidence, Success, Self-Discipline, Productivity, Focus, Self-Esteem, Mental Toughness, Social Intelligence and Leadership Skills

© **Copyright 2019**

All Rights Reserved. No part of this book may be reproduced in any form without permission in writing from the author. Reviewers may quote brief passages in reviews.

Disclaimer: No part of this publication may be reproduced or transmitted in any form or by any means, mechanical or electronic, including photocopying or recording, or by any information storage and retrieval system, or transmitted by email without permission in writing from the publisher.

While all attempts have been made to verify the information provided in this publication, neither the author nor the publisher assumes any responsibility for errors, omissions or contrary interpretations of the subject matter herein.

This book is for entertainment purposes only. The views expressed are those of the author alone, and should not be taken as expert instruction or commands. The reader is responsible for his or her own actions.

Adherence to all applicable laws and regulations, including international, federal, state and local laws governing professional licensing, business practices, advertising and all other aspects of doing business in the US, Canada, UK or any other jurisdiction is the sole responsibility of the purchaser or reader.

Neither the author nor the publisher assumes any responsibility or liability whatsoever on the behalf of the purchaser or reader of these materials. Any perceived slight of any individual or organization is purely unintentional.

Contents

INTRODUCTION 1

CHAPTER 1: 3

CHAPTER 2: 13

CHAPTER 3: 21

CHAPTER 4: 28

CHAPTER 5: 35

CHAPTER 6: 43

CHAPTER 7: 49

CHAPTER 8: 59

CHAPTER 9: 68

CHAPTER 10: 80

CONCLUSION 91

Introduction

In the following chapters, we will discuss:

- The power of positive thinking
- Boosting your confidence
- Skyrocketing your success
- Developing self-discipline
- Improving your productivity
- The importance of harnessing the power of your emotions
- Practical ways to improve your focus
- Tips on how to boost your self-esteem
- Approaching life without apology
- Understanding the importance of setting goals
- Finding ways to become more productive
- Practicing mental toughness
- Social intelligence: Using it to your advantage
- Leadership skills: Effectively manage your life
- Discovering your leadership type…and much more!

If you are struggling with accomplishing your goals, learning your destiny, and tackling life with a positive attitude, then this book is for you! Read on to learn practical ways of ensuring that your future remains bright by harnessing the power of positive thinking and activating the Law of Attraction.

There are plenty of books on this subject; we are glad you chose this one. Please enjoy!

Chapter 1:
The Power of Positive Thinking

When changing your mindset, the first area to address is your thinking processes. Positive thinking helps you in each area of life; when you proactively change how your mind assesses experiences, you begin stepping into a new, better, and brighter future!

- **Living Each Day with Joy**

Each day is a new beginning. Approaching each day with a joyful attitude results in changes. Life begins to look different, bringing positivity into areas in which you have struggled. Below you will find some tips and some strategies to use so that you can approach each day with a joyful attitude and reap the benefits.

- **Don't Wait to Be Happy**

Happiness is your jurisdiction. Your attitude and outlook on life play a major role in determining happiness. If you are waiting for happiness to arrive at your doorstep, you'll be disappointed! It's up to you to *make your happiness.*

- **Seek Happiness Now**

Find something that makes you happy and *pursue it.* Go out on a limb (where the fruit is) and find the results you seek. Making the effort is part of the journey, bringing its own rewards, so resist any tendency to consider the undertaking as anything but positive. Start now!

- **Practice Self-Care**

Meditation, proper nutrition, exercise, and affirmations are examples of how you can practice self-care. Taking care of yourself is a necessary part of growth and maintaining a healthy relationship with yourself, and without it, negativity may creep into your life. Looking after your body and soul is one of the most important tasks in your life.

- **Stop Worrying**

Worrying never accomplishes anything. You cannot seek out happiness if your mind is constantly anxious. Consider journaling about your concerns; seeing them on paper may provide a different perspective, bringing both relief and solutions. Create a habit of proactivity, and you'll not only gain self-confidence, but you'll also be releasing those worries.

- **Be Grateful**

Being grateful helps you understand the good things that you have, shifting your focus away from the things that you don't have. Mindfully thinking about your good fortune increases happiness, filling your days with joy. Begin by making a list of the areas in your life for which you are thankful, listing everything big or small. Reflect on this list and watch how your attitude and perspective changes!

- **Add Positive People to Your World**

Never underestimate the power of positive people. Those we surround ourselves with matter because we pick up on their emotions (or "vibes"), allowing them to affect our energy. If you are always in the company of negative complainers, it will eventually rob you of your peace. Instead, surround yourself with a positive and upbeat crowd which helps you maintain this attitude in yourself. Your joy and happiness should take precedence over negative relationships.

- **Love and Laugh More Often**

Loving yourself becomes easier when you practice loving others. Look for opportunities for displaying affection, forgiveness, empathy, and understanding. Learn to laugh at yourself and laugh with others, increasing happiness for you both. You'll begin experiencing the lasting effects of love and laughter while increasing your positive outlook on life.

- **Create a Bucket List**

A bucket list catalogs everything you wish to accomplish in life; consider it the ultimate list of what you would like to do. For some, it might include climbing Mount Everest; for others, it may be falling in love. Remember that each goal should bring you joy! Making your bucket list a priority is another exercise in self-care because you are making *yourself a* priority, as well.

- **Plan for Happiness**

Remember: ultimately, you control your happiness, and establishing a planned pathway to create joy in your life is another priority. Figure out what brings you joy and create a plan that makes happiness and joy a mainstay in your life. Then proceed on that pathway with a joyful attitude.

Taking Responsibility for Your Present and Future

To adopt a positive mindset, you need to learn to embrace your past, your present, and your future. Taking responsibility for your actions is an effective way to change your life; it is an acknowledgment that you control what your life looks like - both now and in the future.

- **Stop the Blame Game**

Blaming someone else for what has - or has not - happened to you does nothing to help create the life that you want for yourself. Even if a person has brought you harm, releasing blame enables you to move on and embrace a more positive future for yourself.

- **Excuses Don't Help**

Stop making excuses for why you can't do something, why you aren't where you want to be, or any other negative thought. Excuses do nothing to further your goals and entertaining them only holds you back, wasting time and energy that should be spent fulfilling your purpose and achieving happiness. Instead of rationalizing, do something positive and constructive in reaching your goals.

- **Practice Self-Compassion**

Learning to be compassionate with yourself requires forgiving yourself for shortcomings, admitting your weaknesses, and understanding that you cannot do everything. Releasing control of every aspect of your life is the first step on the path towards appropriate self-compassion. You will need to work on this area if you struggle with self-love and self-kindness; success will not come if you don't believe that you deserve value and grace.

- **Accept and Use Your Negative Emotions**

Try as you may to avoid them, negative emotions are part of life. Learning to accept and harness the power of these negative emotions will boost your ability to improve yourself, leading to a happier life. You'll find that negative emotions occur less often, resulting in a more positive outlook on everything you encounter.

- **Find Happiness Internally, Not Externally**

Unhappiness is usually caused by seeking happiness externally. Looking outside yourself for happiness is a trap; find that joy within yourself and notice the change in your thinking patterns. Keeping your focus inward is a way of taking responsibility for who you are and what you do and is an important step towards maturity.

- **Keep Your Word**

Part of accepting and taking responsibility for yourself and your actions starts with keeping your word. If you say you are going to do something, then do it or plan for an alternative that keeps your promise. This is vital to accepting your past, present, and future because if you cannot keep your word, you will never accept responsibility for yourself.

- **Avoid Complaining**

Just like excuses, complaining helps nothing. Complaints take time and energy away from the critical work that you are trying to accomplish, hindering progress towards reaching your goals. We all know someone who bemoans everything in their life. Does that foster a sense of wellbeing in you? Or does it create a feeling of negativity, fueling angst or grief? Try reframing grievances into empowering statements of change. Create a life that does not include complaining!

- **Take Action**

Without taking action, how will you achieve the life that you envision? Shape your present and future by taking control, creating an action plan, and actively tackling any hurdles that stand between you and your goals.

Taking Responsibility for Your Mind and Your Body

Taking responsibility for your mind and your body involves many steps:

- <u>Sleep Well</u> – Take steps to get the right amount of sleep, making sure that the quality of your sleep is good.
- <u>Eat Well</u> – Pay attention to the food you eat, as it fuels your activity. Eating a balanced diet helps your body absorb the necessary nutrients to keep it in tip-top shape. A body fueled on junk food will not give you the results that you desire.

- Exercise - Moderate exercise is going to improve your focus, aid in improving concentration and mood, resulting in a boost of confidence.
- Be Thankful – Mindfully practice a grateful attitude. When you practice gratitude, you will find that not only does your outlook on life change, your perception of the future becomes more positive.
- Take Time to Have Fun - Everyone enjoys a good time, and studies have proven that having fun has positive effects on your life. When you take time to do activities that you enjoy, you are giving your mood a boost, as well as improving how you will tackle the future.
- Avoid Toxic People, Places, and Things - When looking to avoid negativity in your life, the best place to begin is with toxicity. Pinpoint areas in your life where negativity has a foothold, and work to eliminate the influences.
-
- Reflect and Meditate - Take the time to reflect and meditate on your life, your future, and how you plan on reaching the success you desire. If you struggle to calm your mind, find a peaceful place without distractions, and try again.

Shaping your present and your future depends on understanding and mastering each point above. You can - and will - achieve your goals, experiencing the success that you have visualized for yourself.

Tips on Self-Compassion

Self-compassion is essential to living your life with joy and for accepting responsibility for yourself. Below are tips to help you adopt a compassionate mindset.

- **Forgive Yourself**

Everyone makes mistakes, and every mistake offers a way to learn and grow. Self-forgiveness is the greatest gift you can give yourself because it allows you to move forward and shape your future. Just as we forgive others for their past mistakes, choices, or errors, we must release grudges against ourselves. This is the greatest gift, realizing that nothing can change the past, but you can shape your future.

- **Adopt a Growth Mindset**

After granting yourself forgiveness, move towards a mindset that invites and promotes personal growth in terms of your talents and skills. Develop and continue to hone these throughout your life, and you'll experience greater ease in deciding what your future holds. You will be making changes that steer your ship on a course to that future.

- **Be Generous**

Your generosity with others will not only change someone's life but the way *they view their life*. Adopting a grateful attitude is a terrific way to enhance your thinking patterns and those of people around you, setting off good "vibes" for everyone involved.

- **Practice Being Mindful**

Mindfulness means living in the moment, consciously focusing your attention on what is happening around you *as well as within you*. Being mindful of every situation enhances your capacity for compassion.

Control Your Thoughts, Control Your Life

Controlling your thoughts is going to make a huge impact on your life. Once you can control your mind, you'll begin shaping negative thoughts into positive ones.

- **Take a Breath**

When you are experiencing negative thoughts, a good first step is to stop and breathe. By allowing yourself a moment, you are going to find that the situation loses its power. Continue to take deep breaths as you regain your composure and find your footing, allowing your mind to clear and your focus to return. *Do not be afraid to take a moment and practicing deep breathing.* Match your inhaling to your exhaling; this restores calmness and inner peace.

- **Stay Present**

By remaining mindful in the present moment, you cannot fret about the past or the future. You cultivate inner peace by reducing worries, and that's the secret power of remaining present: stay focused on what you can control and release that which you cannot control.

- **Deal in Facts, Not Opinions**

Make sure to look at – and understand - the facts when facing situations where your self-esteem may be in jeopardy. Know what you are good at, understand that you are worthy of good things, and forget about the opinions of others. You may not be viewing yourself in the right light if your self-esteem is suffering. Consider taking an in-depth look at how you view yourself *in light of how others view you.* Establish your own perspective of yourself (practicing self-compassion) and stop worrying about the opinions of others.

- **Address Your Thoughts**

When you find yourself ruminating on negative things, stop and address your thoughts. This prevents your mind from spiraling out of control, allowing you to refine and reform your mindset into a more positive outlook.

- **Find a Comfortable Place**

Finding a comfortable and peaceful place to relax is key to allowing yourself to take control of your thoughts. Be sure that you can remove all distractions that may inhibit a clear, uninterrupted mind.

- **Divert Your Thoughts with Activity**

If you find your thoughts spiraling out of control, try diverting your attention. Find an activity that precludes heavy thinking: helping others, watching a movie, going to an art gallery, etc.

- **Seek Advice for Troubling Thoughts**

When troubling thoughts take over and affect your daily living, seek advice. Gaining an outside perspective often quiets the mind's storm, providing hope and the possibility of resolution.

- **Make Mental Health a Top Priority**

Make sure that you are treating mental health seriously. Relentless negative thinking generally has underlying causes that should be addressed; these thought processes may be arising from an organic imbalance that is easily treatable. Seeking help and advice is always a good idea, especially if you are deeply concerned with your thought life.

Know Your Triggers

When you find yourself dealing with negative thoughts (and the patterns seem repetitive) keep track of what you were doing before these thoughts. Mindfully tracking how and when your thoughts are being shaped will help you identify and avoid triggers. By understanding what triggers these thought patterns, you will then be able to avoid the triggers.

Meditate

Meditation is a form of clearing your mind and gaining control. Meditation can also help realign your thought processes because you are centering yourself and actively choosing to think about other matters.

Understand What You Can - and Can't - Control

By understanding what you can control, you are going to be able to let go of the stuff that you cannot control. Not everything in your life is going to be under your control! When you learn to accept that, you're going to see your thought patterns change. Control what you can and let go of the rest!

Positive thinking is going to reshape your life, and you will see results. People often underestimate the power of positive thinking but implementing this strategy in your life activates the Law of Attraction. We will discuss the Law of Attraction later on in the book but remember that powerful thinking starts by reshaping negative thoughts into positive ones.

Chapter 2
Boost Your Confidence

Your confidence plays a critical role when analyzing your mindset; it also affects the amount of success you can expect from life. By boosting your confidence, you're going to see changes in your thought processes - as well as in your life.

Gaining self-confidence shows that you are in control of your destiny as well is your life. How are some ways that you can tell that you are in control? Below are some examples of how you are in control of your life - and thriving!

If you lose your job, you will be okay. By adopting the right mindset, you will understand that losing your job is not an obstacle or an end of the world situation. Rather, you will view this as an opportunity to change. Losing your job may very well be the kick-start that you needed to start your own business, change career paths, or even move to a different city. When you control your destiny, things like losing your job are not going to send you into a tailspin, but rather they will empower you to change where you are at.

Another example: acting on your instincts in your dating life. Perhaps you are waiting for the right person (and you feel like you found that person), but he or she is unaware of your interest. When you are in control of your life, you understand that it is perfectly acceptable for you to initiate the first encounter, even if it does not feel socially acceptable. Controlling your life includes every area, including your love life. Take action, and don't wait - reach out and grab what you want.

By being in control of your own life, you understand that failure is just part of the journey, accepting them and moving on. The chance to grow as an individual is important – one reason that we face failure. How you handle the failure is going to determine whether you are controlling your life or your life is controlling you. Do not allow yourself to wallow in self-pity! Instead, take control of the situation and rectify it. You know what you want out of life, and no one else is going to give it to you. Take control of your situation and the direction your life is taking – make progress on your own terms.

Owning Who You Are

Part of taking control of your own life and your destiny includes knowing *who you are* and *owning that person*. Accept responsibility for who you are and the actions that you take, and you will see a world of difference in your life. How do you own and accept responsibility for yourself?

- **Accept That You Are a Work-in-Progress**

Each of us grows into the person we wish to be – we are all a work-in-progress! Once you accept the fact that you will not reach perfection, you will find that your perspective on life changes. Continue to learn and grow, understanding that while you may not be perfect, you are evolving into a better person each day.

Explore Who You Are

Self-awareness is a huge part of growing as an individual. Take the time to get to know yourself, understanding your weaknesses, and then learning how those weaknesses shape you as an individual. It's also important to understand what your strengths are and how you can use those to your advantage. Consider journaling to find out what you truly like and don't like, what you are good at, and areas where you may need improvement. The process of self-awareness is going to continue throughout your lifetime.

- **Let Go of What You Cannot Control**

Perhaps you are a person who needs to be in control of every area of their life. You could be experiencing frustration because life continues to throw you curveballs that you have no chance of controlling. Once you understand – then accept – that there are going to be things in your life that you cannot control, you'll find that you are happier and more capable than you first thought. This process increases your self-confidence, as you stop blaming yourself for failures that you have no control over.

- **Face Your Fears**

By facing your fears, you are going to feel better about yourself. Facing your fears does not mean that you overcome them; it means that you understand that you *can continue* even though you are afraid. Pushing through that fear and moving beyond it is an important step towards success.

- **Quiet Your Inner Critic**

Each of us has thoughts running through our heads, seeding doubt that we are not good enough, what we did was stupid, or that we'll never succeed. Thoughts like that come from your inner critic, and you need to learn to silence that voice! Clearly, self-confidence increases when you quit listening to that voice; you will accomplish more, feeling more confident in each task that you take on.

- **Experience Your Emotions, Good or Bad**

We all experience emotions daily. The good emotions seem acceptable, but the bad emotions tend to bring shame. Once you learn to accept that "bad" emotions are okay, you're going to feel better about yourself. Stop attaching negative thoughts to negative emotions! Remember that negative emotions can be driving you to succeed, so embrace the good and the bad.

- **Share Your Vulnerability**

Becoming vulnerable to someone is a huge step. While it may feel like vulnerability is a weakness, it can be viewed as a positive trait. Becoming vulnerable to another individual shows a level of trust – and trust is a critical part of growth. Vulnerability is also important because showing it also reaffirms that you are worthy; this can do wonders for your self-confidence!

- **Find Out How Others View You**

This is a tricky area. While seeking approval from others should never be a high priority, your self-awareness depends partially on sensing how others see you. What do they see as your strengths and your weaknesses? Find out how others view you, taking the feedback as an opportunity to improve, reshaping some weaknesses, and making them into strengths. Never take the opinions of others as fact, but compare how they see you to how you see yourself.

- **Look at the Best Parts of You**

Remember to be proud of aspects of yourself that you like! If you've taken up journaling, make a list of your characteristics or accomplishments that make you feel successful. Write down your strengths and make a point to focus on this at least once a day. These daily affirmations will go a long way in building your self-confidence and reminding you that you are worthy of self-praise.

Make Your Destiny – Plan Your Ideal Future

You must understand that you are in control of your destiny and that you can *(and should)* shape your future. Once you embrace this truth, you'll see that your choices take on new importance.

This can become an exciting part of self-growth! Take the time to develop a vision for your future and then plan for that future. Write down your dreams and what you hope to accomplish. Dream big, understanding that you can do whatever you set your mind to and no one can hold you back. If you accept the power within to form your future, you can map it out, and run with it!

- **Be Realistic**

Realism and practicality do play a part in your future, and limitations do exist. That said, don't allow yourself to dwell on what you can't do though. Instead, apply realistic thinking, consider appropriate timeframes for reaching your goals. For example, it may be fun to consider losing 100 pounds in 30 days, but it's also unrealistic (and dangerous!) Give yourself a break – be realistic!

- **Understanding Your Passion**

While moving towards the goal line, remind yourself *who you are working for!* Whose goals are you trying to reach: your own, or someone else's? Don't lose focus on your own goals and the skills it takes to reach them. While you may be doing someone else's work for them, remind yourself daily about your future goals and how your daily life moves you closer to reaching them. Your passion fuels your daily work, and your daily work is moving you closer to reaching your goals. If you find that you are moving through days without passion, stop to consider where your focus lies: yourself or others?

- **Honesty**

Be honest with yourself about what you can accomplish. Do you have the drive that it takes and have you developed the passion that you need to succeed? Honestly look at what you are good at, what you are passionate about, and how all of these can play a part in your future. Often, we overlook our passion when considering our future, forgetting that a passionless life drains confidence. The world tells us we must march along, working only for others, and leaving our future in their hands, not our own! Apply honesty regarding your skills and goals, but remember that passion should be fueling your travels, not solely necessity or other people's goals.

- **Consider Your Tools and Resources**

When shaping your destiny and taking control of your life, you must assess the tools and resources available to take you to your desired future. What skills do you have readily available? Are you actively honing those skills in anticipation of the day that you get to reach out and take control? Again, making a list will help you scrutinize those abilities, tools, and resources as you make your way in life.

- **Ignore the Critics**

You will face critics throughout your life; there will always be someone saying you cannot do something. Remember that others' opinions are just that: opinions. Hearing critical voices is different than *listening to them!* Often critics have met with failure in their own lives, and they are just projecting that failure onto your life. Don't give them the power to tear down your self-confidence!

- **Settle for Nothing Less than Excellence**

Settling for mediocrity leads you down a dead-end path. Striving for excellence, reshaping your thought processes, understanding that you are worthy of a bright future; that mindset takes you to success. Affirm your self-worth daily, remembering that you do not deserve mere adequacy – you deserve excellence!

Tips to Boost Your Confidence

This chapter has been all about your self-confidence and how it's going to help you be in control of your life and take control of your destiny. What if you don't feel great about yourself? How do you go about boosting your self-confidence and loving who you are?

Choose to Accept You

If you do not accept to you are, then others sense that, making it difficult for them to accept you. Learning to love yourself is the first step in boosting your self-confidence! Remember to quell the critics; just because somebody else thinks something is wrong with you *does not make them right*. Embrace your quirks and your idiosyncrasies and love yourself despite what anyone else tells you. While you may be a work-in-progress, you are moving towards perfection. In the interim, be humble where you may lack luster, and take advantage of your naturally good characteristics to shine!

Perfectionism – a Fallacy

Do not fall for the false assumption that you need to be – or can be – perfect. Understanding that simple concept frees you to accept that how you are - right now - is good enough. Embracing this idea allows you to be happier with yourself. This does not mean that you ignore weaknesses, limitations, or faults; being aware of these is the only way to begin overcoming them. We cannot change what we do not know. That said, letting go of perfectionism boosts your self-confidence, enabling you to embrace everything about what makes you unique.

Understand the Confidence Within

Have you ever felt the glimmer of confidence in something that you have done utterly well? Do you allow that small flame to engulf every part of who you are, or do you extinguish that flame? Perhaps you've had confidence within you but felt that it was somehow wrong to embrace it. Find the confidence within you and allow that light to shine! There is greatness within you – it should be received enthusiastically. Dig deep and discover the confidence you already have and watch your life change for the better.

- **Ignore Your Inner Critic**

Earlier in the chapter, we discussed quieting your inner critic – no one needs to have a constant negative voice telling them they are not good enough. We are our own worst critic. No one else is going to be as hard on you as you are on yourself, and you need to stop this pattern. Understanding that you can reshape your thoughts and quiet the critic will send your confidence soaring. If we have outside negative voices attacking us every day, do we need to add our voice to the mix? Consider that question. If you are listening to the outside, taking to heart every bad comment, your inner voice and inner thoughts will mirror that sentiment. Calm and ignore your inner critic. Nothing beneficial is going to come from you criticizing yourself. Simply put: love yourself enough to close your ears to negativity within.

Ask for Help

Perhaps you don't know - or cannot accept – that you are worthy. Do not feel afraid to ask for help from someone that you trust (a friend or a professional.) Sometimes we need to have another person validate what we are feeling. Find someone that you trust and that you can be honest with to help you sort through who you are.

Dwell on the Positive, Not the Negative

Focus on the positive and forget the negative. That is easier said than done, but it is something that you need to strive for. When you concentrate on looking for positives, that's what you begin to see all around you (and it works with negatives, as well!) Optimism is a great trait to embrace as it leads to a happier and more successful life. It is your choice, take control and mindfully choose to dwell on the positive aspects of every day, making a mental note of them as you fall asleep. Those obstacles that you faced on your way to a promotion? No problem! Those were just road signs to improvement. Choosing how you view everything that happens puts you in control of your confidence – or lack of confidence.

Your confidence is an essential part of who you are, and in the face of a world of negativity, your success depends on your ability to understand the correlation between confidence and success in life. You are in control of your destiny; your life does not control you. Take time to work on your self-confidence if you struggle in this area. You are worthy, and you are important. Never forget that you deserve happiness and greatness.

Chapter 3
Success and You

Most people want to be successful in life, and I imagine you are one of those people. You picked up this book, didn't you? This shows you are willing to put the work in to make yourself successful. Success depends on many factors: how you approach the obstacles in life, how you live life, and how you tackle problems – all these determine the level of success that you experience.

Live Life on Your Terms

You do not need the validation of someone else to feel important or to feel worthy of success. Learning to live life on your terms is a huge step and will not only allow you to experience success, but it will also allow you to do what you want and what you love without the validation of someone else.

- ### Dream A Little or A Lot

Your dreams are important, and they are a vital part of your success. Give yourself a chance to dream and embrace the life that you want. Let your mind wander, journal about your dreams, and set out to make them a reality. Dreaming is not only allowed, but it is also encouraged! Our dreams determine what we need to be doing in life; without them, we flounder.

- **Consider Your Reality**

Take a moment and understand where you are at in your life. Take stock of your reality now and taking steps to better yourself becomes your path into the life you've envisioned for yourself. What changes do you need to make to help you achieve your goals? How do you need to approach life so that you can reach where you want to be? Understanding where you are at in life, what you want, and how to get there is important.

- **Think, but Don't Dwell, About the Past**

What choices have you made in the past that have either advanced where you want to be or hindered your progress? Take some time to think about where you have been so that you can take steps to get where you want to be. Your past does not define you, but learning from obstacles you've faced is an important part of living life on your terms and shaping your life into what you want it to be. Do not allow yourself to criticize your past, but objectively ponder where you have been.

- **Check Your Options**

Understand the options that are available to you. By doing this, you are going to know where you can go in life and how to get there. Perhaps you need to make some changes at the moment to get you where you need to go. If you desire to live in Paris, but your bank account is empty, perhaps you need to make some money and learn some skills to keep you afloat once you get to Paris. Understanding the options that are available to you is important so that you can take steps to get you where you desire.

- **Seek Advice**

Advice is important only if it comes from somebody that you trust. Listening to those who truly do not have your best interests at heart is dangerous; they may seek to tear you down rather than build you up. A trusted friend or professional is likely to provide constructive feedback, helping you reach your goals. Seek advice from somebody who has already achieved what you are trying to achieve and who can help you understand the process. Understanding how they got to where you want to be is beneficial so that you can mimic their success. The steps that they have taken are going to give you guidelines and help you avoid common pitfalls.

- **Make a Plan**

For some people, planning is fun – others despise it! Having a plan is a good idea when you are looking to make your life what you wanted to be. When you have a plan, you are going to know if you are on the right path. Without a plan, you could end up thinking you're on the right path, but then fail to succeed.

- **Take Action**

Nothing happens without effort, and that includes achieving your goals. To live life on your terms and achieve the goals that you have set for yourself, you must act. Once you've made a plan, set out to make that plan a reality. The effort that you put into your goals and the journey that you take is often as (or more) important than the result. Have confidence that you are going to succeed, but if you miss the mark, take action to correct where you went wrong.

- **Law of Attraction**

The Law of Attraction states that the power of the universe is going to help you manifest the life that you want. In applies to thoughts, ideas, people, situations, and circumstances. The Law of Attraction allows you to manifest whatever it is you desire.

Goal Setting

Your goals are important, and you need to set goals for your life. Once you have set your goals, you have a plan to get the life that you want. Remember that your goals should motivate you; if they fail to inspire you to action, consider taking another look! A side note on motivation: sometimes you need to get started to *feel that motivation!*

- **Your Goals Should Be Smart**

Smart means specific, measurable, attainable, relevant, and timely. Each of your goals should meet these requirements and if they don't, reframe them so that they do. When you follow these smart guidelines, you increase the chances of meeting your goals.

- **Write Them Down**

Write down your goals and keep that list in a place you can see them daily (refrigerator, car dash, work desk.) Keeping the list within visual range is important, helping you remember what you are doing and what you are working for. Be sure to express them with positive wording and use a to-do list to accomplish the steps that you need to take to be successful.

- **Take Action**

You've probably noticed that "take action" is a recurrent theme throughout this book. Goals without action or effort are useless. If you need to, break them down into smaller steps and use the steps to show you when you are on the right track. The steps are merely guidelines that are going to allow you to track your progress. Put effort into your goals; that effort will never be wasted.

- **Don't Give Up**

No matter what life throws you, never give up on your goals. The only way that you can fail is if you concede defeat. Your goals should be important enough to you that no matter what you face, you will not give up. Cling to the idea that quitting is not an option because your life is within your control and you will do whatever is needed to be successful.

Face Your Fears – Know They are Normal.

Your fears can become an obstacle to starting your climb to success and can be a powerful enemy – or a powerful motivator. As a natural part of life, fear can present a challenge that you meet, an enemy you can beat. Don't allow yourself to get caught up in cycles of fear. Face fears, identify the culprit and work through the experience. Remember that we all face fears; what you do with them defines courage. Allow yourself to become paralyzed into inaction, and fear wins. Acting bravely and moving forward is for winners!

- **Obstacles? No, Opportunities!**

Reframe your thought processes to view obstacles as reasons to grow rather than reasons to stop. A good way to view obstacles is to look at them as a yield sign in life. A yield sign means that you need to slow down and look around you. Once you get a picture of the environment around you, are free to go or make it changes as necessary. Obstacles do not mean that you need to stop altogether or that you are on the wrong path; they are just simple ways for you to change direction or grow as an individual.

- **Negative Feedback Is a Suggestion**

Negative feedback is important to show you ways that you need to improve. Sometimes the feedback is hard to hear, but when you train yourself to look at it as a suggestion, you will have an easier time with it. When you hear negative feedback, listen to the message, and look for ways to improve. Feel free to offer your feedback to whoever is speaking to you, helping them understand that reframing what they have to say may be important, as well.

- **Commit to Improving**

Improvement should always be your goal. This is a lifelong goal that deserves a positive commitment to success!

- **Set Small Goals**

Small goals are going to make success easier – they are the equivalent of taking baby steps. If you have large goals, break them down into smaller, more manageable steps. Track your progress so that you can look back and see how far you've come.

- **Be Accountable**

An accountability partner is a good option because when you have someone who is monitoring your progress with you, you are less likely to let them down. Another way to be held accountable is to let others know the goals that you have for yourself. Once you've made your goals known to others, you've created one more element of motivation in terms of reaching those goals.

- **Motivate Yourself**

The funny thing about motivation is that sometimes you need to get going to feel motivated. Take the first step and get yourself psyched up about the goals that you're trying to achieve. By doing this, you're going to see what you are capable of and you can keep yourself motivated by seeing the progress that you're making.

- **Keep Going, Despite Setbacks**

Setbacks are bound to happen, and if you have a plan of how to handle them, you're going to be able to keep going and maintain your progress. Don't let a setback stop you! Instead, take a moment, discover the cause, and change direction as needed. Remember that the only true failure is quitting.

Successful Relationships

To be successful in life, you need to understand how relationships work and how to hone your "people skills." Perhaps you're not a people person; you still need to learn what makes relationships successful and how to have positive interactions with people. When you improve those important skills, you'll find that your relationships are richer and more rewarding.

- **What Are Your Relationship Needs?**

Make sure to identify your own needs in a relationship. Yes, the needs of the other person are important, but your needs are important as well. If you are not getting what you need out of a relationship, let the other person know, and be willing to let the relationship end.

- **Make Time to Build Relationships**

Sometimes life gets busy. It takes time and effort to build and maintain relationships, and if you aren't able or willing to nurture them, they die on the vine. Always look for ways to build new relationships, because the connections that you have with other individuals are going to play a vital role in how you view yourself - and your success. Keep in mind that everyone enjoys feeling valued, appreciated, and cared for, but they'll never know if you don't take the time and effort to show it! Find creative ways to show that you are keeping up with their life, that their accomplishments matter, and that they play a significant role in your life.

- **Maintain a Positive Attitude**

You'll hear this a lot in this book, as well: build and maintain an adventurous, ambitious, and positive attitude! Your relationships will thrive because no one likes to hang around with a downer.

- **Set Boundaries**

While positive relationships are important, you must set boundaries for those around you, letting them know what you are willing to do, when you are available, what you will tolerate, and what you expect from them. This goes for work and personal relationships. Otherwise, your time and energy are not being preserved.

Chapter 4

A combination of focus and self-discipline is the grease that keeps the success-engine running smoothly. Both are skills you should develop and strengthen.

Tips for Self-Discipline

Self-discipline is a powerful tool in achieving success and reaching your goals. A critical by-product is finding that your determination has deepened, and your motivation is fueled. Here are some tips to improve your self-discipline.

- **Acknowledge Your Weaknesses**

While we all have weaknesses, those who acknowledge them have taken the first step towards improving their self-discipline. You cannot change what you don't see; failing to bring light to your weaknesses is a sure hindrance on your path to success. Once you've identified weaknesses, remember to commit to taking consistent action to improve those areas of your life.

- **Avoid Temptations**

Once you've identified your weaknesses, look for patterns (or triggers) that launch the temptation to succumb to that shortcoming. Again – if you can't see it, you can't stop it! By determining the exact provocation or trigger, you may begin to see these temptations differently. Given a chance to avoid them altogether, you will see your self-discipline and willpower increase. Don't forget: mindfully creating a list of weaknesses and triggers for temptation (and placing them in view) will help avoid situations that challenge your willpower.

- **Have Clear Expectations**

Know what you expect and what you must do to achieve your goals. If you are unsure of your expectations, how can you know when they've been fulfilled? Take time to clearly identify what you are trying to achieve as well as how you plan on getting to that destination?

- **Practice Self-Discipline - It Doesn't Come Naturally**

No one is born with self-discipline; like a muscle, it must be exercised! When you see others reaching their goals through self-mastery, remember that this was their decision, not a magical destiny. Knowing it requires efforts from us all may be key to helping you remain steadfast in reaching your goals.

- **Create Positive Habits**

Be mindful (starting today) of your habits, the routines that you follow, and the patterns that are part of your life. Determine which habits move you towards your goals, and which move you away from your goals. Make a plan to eliminate the unhelpful habits, and an equally strong plan to incorporate positive habits into your routine, making them a part of who you are.

- **Nutrition Is Important**

This one is simple: It's hard to maintain self-discipline when your body is feeble; nutrition is key to feeling your strongest and best. Make proper nutrition a priority in your life!

- **Willpower May Not Be What You Think**

Willpower is your ability to avoid temptations and triggers, doing what you know is crucial to your success – even when you don't feel like it. What is your idea of willpower? Perhaps you have misconceptions about willpower and self-discipline; take a closer look to see if you are seeing these traits in the best light possible.

- **Have A Plan B**

There will be times your willpower or self-discipline is weak. Having a backup plan provides a way back to the path when you are temporarily lost – before your plan goes over the cliff entirely! Give yourself a chance to rectify the situation, allowing yourself grace, forgiveness, and an opportunity to try again without starting a square one again.

- **Reward progress**

Keep track of the progress that you are making and reward yourself when your willpower shines. Soon the rewards become bonuses rather than motivation. When you track the progress that you are making, you can see for yourself exactly what you have accomplished. It's easy to forget the progress that you have made, and by visually registering your forward track, you self-validate and enhance your capacity for self-discipline.

- **Forgive and Move On, Be Kind to Yourself**

Everyone needs forgiveness at some point in their life. Often, we are harder on ourselves than others, withholding forgiveness for silly reasons. Perhaps you feel that if you punish yourself for slipping and making a mistake, you'll move faster towards your goals later. This is a myth, and you are more likely to improve yourself if you offer forgiveness rather than punishment. Remember to practice self-compassion as you move towards improving yourself!

Tips for Focus

Maintaining focus on our path and goal is an essential element to success, but too often an element we fail to master. Improving your focus keeps you on task, ensuring that you accomplish everything you set out to accomplish in life. Here are some tips to help you build and improve your focus.

- **Exercise**

Regular exercise frees your mind of the clutter life sends your way, helping you focus better. Decluttering one's thoughts and keeping one's body healthy are essential traits of a person who is determined to reach their goals.

- **Stay Hydrated**

Along with exercise and proper nutrition, it's important to remember to stay hydrated. Drinking enough water helps your brain function better. Besides, if you are dehydrated, you'll be distracted with what your body needs and not the task at hand. It's better to avoid the distraction by making sure that you get the proper amount of water for your body.

- **Look at What Is Important in Life**

What's important to you in life is going may look very different than what's important to someone else. Make sure that you identify what is important to you and focus on that. Everything else is either a distraction or a benefit, but your focus should remain on what you value. By focusing on what you value most, you are allowing yourself to let go of the distractions, which will improve your focus.

- **Avoid Distractions**

Distractions are everywhere in life, and you are probably already aware of those that grab your attention the most. Perhaps you are distracted by your phone. If this is the case, then you need to make sure that you put your phone away when you have important tasks to accomplish. Leave it across the room, hide it in a drawer - do whatever you need to ensure that you are going to be able to stay on task. Keep a list of what distracts you, and before you begin working, take some time to put those distractions away. When you regularly do this, you are going to see an improvement in your focus.

- **Stop Multitasking**

Multitasking is a horrible idea. Multitasking accomplishes nothing other than spreading your focus thinly over several projects. None of the projects are going to get accomplished with great detail because you're not giving each one the full attention it deserves. Make it a habit to focus on one task or activity at a time; you'll soon discover your ability to complete the objective much faster and better.

- **Small Steps**

Rome was not built in a day, and neither is your focus going to be improved in one sitting. Set small goals and take small steps that are going to help you in the long run. Each small advancement is an accomplishment, and you should be proud of it. Do not expect gigantic leaps, but rather focus on the small steps in progress that you're making. When you are worrying about making large advancements, your focus is going to be off. Become used to taking small steps, and leave the big ones for giants.

- **Refocus as Needed**

When you lose focus, take a moment, and breathe. From there, refocus and get back to work. Do not berate yourself; distraction is a human condition. Acknowledge your humanness, refocus, and move on.

Tips for Meditation

Meditation is an effective way to build your concentration and focus. A lovely by-product is a reduction in stress levels! Below you'll find some tips for meditation.

- **Designated Space**

Have a space reserved solely for your meditation time. This area should remain free of distractions and negative energy. By reserving this special area, your body will learn that when you are there, your mind is free, and your inner being is ready. In time, you will begin to crave your designated space and meditation time.

- **Make Time**

Setting aside time for this special, positive habit is an important step towards re-energizing your spirit within, improving your overall health, focus, and concentration. Clear a spot in your schedule and make this a routine every day (if possible). Just after waking and just before bedtime are both good times to practice meditation, as you are most relaxed and better able to lose yourself in meditation.

- **Start a Routine**

Routines involve structuring your day in such a way that you avoid unnecessary decisions, preparing your body prepared for the needed work. When you are on autopilot, you will find that simple tasks are easier and simple decisions do not take extra thought. When you start a routine that involves meditation, you find that your body is programmed to anticipate this activity – and you feel more prepared. Your body is going to start to relax before the anticipated meditation time, and this allows your mind to wander fully.

- **Get Comfortable**

Change comfortable and non-restricting clothes, giving your body the chance to relax and experience the full benefits of meditation. Sit in a comfortable position, perhaps using pillows or mats to soften the effects of a hard surface. That said, don't get *too* comfortable or you may fall asleep!

- **Breathe**

As you begin your meditative state, pay attention to your breathing. Breathe in through your nose and exhale through your mouth. Make sure that the inhale lasts as long as the exhale. Keep a rhythm to your breathing, and breathe deeply. Breathing is an important part of meditating, and it allows your body to relax.

- **Let Your Mind Wander**

As you are breathing and you are feeling your body relax, let your mind wander. Do not allow yourself to stop the flow of thoughts but embrace each one that comes your way. Allowing your mind to wander reduces inhibitions, allowing your body to relax further, releasing your need to control other parts of your life at this important time of recharging.

Meditation is great to help you improve your discipline and your focus. Giving yourself the time and space to meditate (releasing control) actually improves your ability to maintain control during the parts of the day that require your utmost attention.

Further Reading Suggestions:

The Miracle of Mindfulness: An Introduction to the Practice of Meditation

By: Thich Nat Hahn

How to Meditate: A Practical Guide

By: Kathleen MacDonald

The Myth of Freedom and The Way of Meditation

By: Chugiak Trongsa

Chapter 5

You have your goals set, you have your mindset in positive mode, but now you need actually to get to work. How in the world do you keep yourself productive when it feels like you have too much to do, but not enough time to accomplish these tasks? Productivity is important to achieve your goals, and below, you will find tips, techniques, and strategies to help increase productivity in your life.

Beat Procrastination and Embrace Productivity

Procrastinating is the enemy. At all costs, you need to avoid procrastination so that you can embrace productivity and increase your positive outcomes.

• **Breakdown Your Work into Smaller Steps**

A common theme with mindset, productivity, and achieving success in life is *small steps*. Baby steps are important to achieving your goals because when you take on too much, you run the risk of becoming overwhelmed. By becoming overwhelmed, you run the risk of giving up, leading to failure. Small steps allow you to tackle your goals and projects without feeling overwhelmed. Do not underestimate how quickly small steps add up because if you do, you are going to miss beautiful parts of the journey.

- **Be Mindful of Your Work Environment**

Your productivity is affected by the environment that you're working in. Clutter, color, air quality, and temperature can all affect your productivity. Pay attention to how cluttered your workstation is, because clutter tells your brain that more work needs to be done, and you will never fully focus on the task before you. Color can affect not only your mood but your productivity as well. Boring colors (such as browns and whites) are going to make you feel sluggish and tired. Bright or bold colors may cause your mind to race rather than focus. Air quality and temperature are important as well; when these are inadequate, you become focused on your physical comfort rather than the work ahead of you. Take some time to adjust your surroundings to optimize your productivity.

- **Set Detailed Timelines**

Sometimes we like to be vague in the deadlines that we set because we feel like we can get more accomplished if we are not pinned down by a specific timeline. Don't fall into this trap, because when you set detailed timelines and expectations, you are going to be more productive overall. Your timelines should include deadlines for each step of your task, project, or activity. Ensure that you are staying focused and on time by keeping these timelines within easy reach (within sight is even better!)

- **Identify Triggers for Procrastination**

You know what triggers you to procrastinate, and when you are honest with yourself and identify these triggers if you are going to see your productivity increase. Falling victim to these triggers only hurts yourself. Make and keep a list of known procrastination triggers, trying to avoid them when you need to be productive. Some examples of triggers could be your phone ringing, notifications being sent on your phone, or others dropping by unexpectedly. Make a decision and a choice to keep yourself away from these triggers and placing value on reaching your goals. Productivity is a skill, and you need to strengthen and hone it just like other skills.

- **Surround Yourself with Productive People**

The people you surround yourself with *do affect* your productivity. One example might be your spouse working at home with you; you may feel the need to catch up and chat often. Make a point of isolating yourself from people who distract you. By surrounding yourself with productive people who are busily pursuing their own goals, you are ensuring that you are setting yourself up for success rather than failure. Mimic the productive efforts of others around you, ingraining their good habits into your daily routine.

- **Broadcast Your Goals**

Your goals are important to you, and you should let others know about them. Broadcasting your goals is a way of having others hold you accountable, driving you to be productive and reach your goals. Sometimes just not wanting to disappoint others is a good way to increase your productivity.

- **Seek Advice**

Helpful and constructive advice is something that you should always seek. By looking for help, you are giving yourself a chance to learn new techniques and strategies that are going to help you achieve your desired results.

- **Don't Over Complicate Things**

Are you a person who somehow makes the simplest task complicated? Creating impediments kills motivation and productivity! Keep everything as simple as you can and see how much more successful you are. By over-complicating things, you are giving yourself an excuse to quit. Remember, we discussed that you need to get rid of excuses to be successful. Simple and effective is the way to go; you'll see your success skyrocket because your productivity increases.

- **Pick A Point and Start**

The most important part of any journey is the beginning. But where to start? If you have written down where you are, where you need to be, and how to get there – then start where you are and take the first step towards getting to Point B. Perhaps you need to sign up for an online class, buy a how-to book, or call a successful mentor and ask for help. Get started, or you will achieve nothing. If you are nervous about starting, you may be fearful of failure. If so, identify the fear, and commit to moving beyond it. Maybe you don't start because you fear an imperfect result. In this case, your starting point is ridding yourself of the perfection myth! Pick a spot and begin, remembering that without a start, the only ending is failure.

Productivity Tips and Techniques

Everyone can use a hand when it comes to learning new ways to be effective. Below you will find tips and techniques that are going to help you skyrocket your productivity and achieve the success that you want.

- **Don't Multitask**

Multitasking should no longer be a part of your vocabulary and shall no longer be part of your work patterns. Multitasking requires you to tackle more than one project or activity at a time. This results in a poor quality of work, less productivity, and loss of focus. If you want to increase your productivity, learn how to hyper-focus on one task at a time. See how much more you get accomplished when you are not spreading your focus across multiple tasks.

- **Take A Break**

Everyone needs a break when they're working on something. When you try to push through without breaks, you're harming your productivity. Think about a task that you do and then think about the times that you pause and daydream. Are you accomplishing anything, or are you just wasting time? These are important patterns to notice because essentially, you are taking a break, but they are not productive breaks. A productive break allows you to recharge your battery and maintain your focus. Take a walk, stretch, or get something to drink. Remember that breaks do not decrease productivity, but they increase it.

- **Small Goals Are Best**

This is another one of those common themes throughout this book! Large goals are beautiful to look at, and the big picture is amazing. However, completing large goals is complicated. Remember we said that it's best not to set complicated expectations because when you do this, you run the risk of giving up before you even begin. Break each large goal into smaller goals and monitor your progress this way. Small steps allow you to get more accomplished.

- **Use Your Most Productive Time for Important Tasks**

Each of us has time during the day that we are more productive. Pinpointing and using that time to your advantage is important. Some people work better in the mornings, accomplishing more in a few early hours than the whole afternoon. Others prefer afternoons or even late-night hours. Then there are the night owls who get more done while others are sleeping! Listening to your body and your biological clock is going to allow you to utilize the time of day that works best for you.

Reorganize Your Life and Work

To be productive, it's important to revitalize your workspace and make organization a priority. To be successful and productive, make appropriate use of the space that you have available. Below you will find some tips to reorganize your working life and increase productivity.

- **Organize Your Time**

Organizing your time is going to revitalize how you approach life. By knowing what you must do and when you have to do it, you're giving yourself a structured routine which - in the end - frees up your time. Block off the amount of time that tasks are going to take and only work on those tasks during that timeframe. It's important to schedule everything; when you have something written in your schedule, you are more likely to finish.

- **Enforce Time Limits on Work**

Remember the old proverb: "All work and no play makes Jack a dull boy." When you are only focused on working, you're going to burn yourself out, decreasing productivity. Allow time away from work to help you maintain a clear mind and motivation to succeed. If you end up running over your timeframe for working, make it a point to find time elsewhere in your schedule to have time set aside for yourself.

- **Maintain a Work Environment**

Take the appropriate measures to ensure that your environment is designated as an *only-work* environment. Don't allow yourself to intertwine tasks or activities into space. Like meditation, keeping an environment solely for working is a way of programming your body and your mind to understand that the space is specific to a specific task. This is an effective way to separate your mind away from work if you happen to work from home. Your office space should be separate from your other space. This increases your productivity because you do not feel distracted by the other stuff that could be going on instead.

- **Set Times to Check Emails and Phone Calls**

Have designated times -twice daily - to check your emails and return phone calls. If you're constantly checking your emails, this is a distraction and decreases your productivity. Phone calls also tend to be a distraction, as well. If you can, avoid taking phone calls and instead return them at the time you designate. Increasing your productivity requires that you stay on task and you avoid distractions.

- **Keep a To-Do List**

To-do lists often get bad reputations, but they are appropriate and useful, reminding you of what you need to accomplish. Keep a running list, but only designate five priorities for each day; more than five may run the risk of spreading yourself too thin or becoming distracted by other tasks that needing your attention. If five priorities are too much, consider breaking that down to three.

- **Check Your Mindset**

Maintaining a positive mindset is so important; losing that confident outlook can prevent you from being productive. Negativity should have no place in the new life that you are trying to build. If you find yourself losing momentum – examine your current mindset. Are you suffering from negative thought processes, or perhaps you received some negative feedback, and now you are questioning everything that you have accomplished? Take time each day to make sure that your mindset is appropriate and that you are looking at things optimistically. Remember, perfection is a myth, being productive is not!

- **Affirmations**

Affirmations are positive statements that you repeat to yourself daily. The statements invoke the Law of Attraction, allowing you to manifest positivity into your life. Affirmations should be spoken in the morning, and you need to make sure that you believe them! Embrace the power in telling yourself that positivity shall prevail and remind yourself that you can take action as well. Coincidences have no place in your life; what happens to you happens for a reason.

- **Visualize Your and Result**

Visualization is an effective way to increase your productivity and change your mindset. By visualizing the result that you desire, you can then implement any needed changes to your routine. Visualize your result and experience the emotions that come along with it.

This makes the vision feel real, increasing the likelihood of your desired outcome.

- **Manage Your Paperwork**

Getting a strong hold on paperwork can be a challenge and maintaining that stronghold can be even harder! Allowing paperwork to accumulate and clutter your work area reduces productivity. The same applies to emails. Below are some tips to help you keep your paperwork organized and eliminate the clutter and stress associated with it.

- Regularly purge unnecessary paperwork
- Use a color-coded system
- Have a mail station
- Use labels
- Categorize
- Organize other office items

Your productivity is affected by numerous factors, but by exercising care in your environment, your health, and your mindset will put you on a path to success!

Chapter 6

During this chapter, we are going to delve further into your focus and concentration. Focus is vital to success, and you must understand how to concentrate. Dividing your attention between too many tasks is a hurdle you can avoid. In this chapter, we will discuss ways to improve her concentration and focus, the benefits of reading more, and some practical exercises which help eliminate distractions and improve your focus.

Improve Your Concentration and Focus

There are several effective tips and strategies to adopt when you are trying to improve your focus and concentration. Try a mixture of techniques, using what works best for you.

- **Rest**

Rest is vital to each area of your life. By making sure that you have enough rest, you are setting yourself up to be successful and achieve your goals; this goes for your mindset, as well. If you are not tired or sluggish, your focus and your concentration suffer, finding that maintaining a positive mindset is difficult. Make sure that you are going to bed at a reasonable time, and that you are sticking with a schedule in terms of when you get awaken each day. Keeping the routine is going to ensure that your body knows when it's time to rest. Avoiding caffeine too late in the day is another good way to make sure that your body rests when it is time to retire at night.

- **Have a Plan**

Plans are important, contributing to your concentration and focus, assisting you in understanding how to tackle any problems that come your way. Include plans to ensure that your workplace is free of distractions which can lead to wasted time and energy.

- **Control Your Diet**

Diet and exercise are important. Proper nutrition is part of improving focus and concentration. Vitamins and supplements have been shown to increase concentration, and you can also ask your physician which steps may help with focus. Supplements such as fish oil and omega-3 have been proven to increase your attention span; there are special supplements for individuals who have ADHD and ADD.

- **Mix Up Your Work Environment**

Where you physically do your work influences concentration, as mentioned in chapter five. Take time to look around your workplace with an eye for eliminating distractions, keeping temperatures comfortable, considering lighting (Is it too bright? Too dim?) Incorporating nature light improves your mood and helps with productivity. Take some time to look around your work environment – make changes that improve how you feel in your own workspace. Perhaps what worked yesterday isn't going to work a week from now, and that's okay. Just take the time to understand how your environment is affecting your focus.

- **Practice**

While it may sound silly to suggest that you should practice your focus and concentration, this is how you improve it. How do bodybuilders get their muscle and strength? They take steps to train their bodies. You can practice focus while meditating. Take time each day to practice controlling your thoughts and redirecting where your thoughts take you. This is a good way to practice focusing and concentration because you are willing yourself to follow a regimented plan. Incorporate time into your daily routine for practicing focus; soon, your body and mind will understand when it's time to focus and when it's okay to let your thoughts wander.

- **Read More, Watch Less**

Reading will enhance your ability to focus and concentrate. Screen time, such as your phone, tablet, computer, and television, disrupts your cognitive functions. Find books that you enjoy and start turning pages; the benefits of reading are amazing.

- **Mental Stimulation**

Reading stimulates your mind. When watching television, you are focusing on the screen – not working your brain. It's important to stimulate your mind because, without it, you're going to lose skills valuable and vital skills such as problem-solving and vocabulary. Your memory will fade faster without mental stimulation.

- **Reduces Stress**

Reading is a great way to reduce stress. Allowing yourself to be lost in a book is a good way to forget about the problems plaguing you.

- **Gain Knowledge**

Books are written each day on every subject imaginable. If you're not a person who enjoys fiction, nonfiction is a great way to work your mind and learn new things. Gaining knowledge should always be a goal for you because life is about continually learning. Do not underestimate the value of a good book. Within the pages of books lie the answers to questions that you would normally ask Google!

- **Improve Your Vocabulary**

Everyone can stand to learn more words, improve their vocabulary, and become a better conversationalist. Your vocabulary and skills at expression say a lot about your knowledge, and you can enhance any conversation by being more articulate. No one says that you must learn big words to look knowledgeable, but rather, it's important to be able to employ diverse words to express your ideas. Having a diverse vocabulary will take you far in life.

- **Improve Your Memory**

If you struggle with memory, start reading and watch your memory improve. The mental stimulation that you have when you read is also increasing your ability to remember.

- **Strengthens Analytical Skills**

Being analytical is a valuable skill to have; gaining all your knowledge from television does nothing to develop your analytical skills. Learning to pore through literature or reference materials leads to adroitness and sharper mental acuity. By reading, you are improving those skills rather than tearing them down.

- **Improves Writing and Communication Skills**

Your written and communication skills are used every day of your life. Writing is valuable in most professions because it seems everybody needs to write a report, fill out applications, or perform various written tasks. Communication skills are vital in your relationships, your work, and everyday life. Being able to communicate effectively both in written and verbal form is to serve you well in your path to success.

Practical Exercises to Eliminate Distractions

Perhaps you're wondering how you can improve your focus by eliminating distractions; you may need some exercises or techniques! Eliminating distractions is going to help you concentrate on what's in front of you.

- **Turn Off Your Devices**

Your phone, tablet, and television are distractions. If you are not using any of the above for your work, turn them off and put them away. In this day and age, technology is vital to what individuals are doing. Consider other ways that you're able to complete your work if you find that you are continually distracted by the technology that you are required to use. There are apps to block sites such as social media, email; lose those distractions! Earlier, we mentioned that you should have a time limit on when and how long you can check your email and answer phone calls. This is also applicable to checking social media sites. The Internet can guzzle your time and steal your focus. By turning off your devices, you are giving yourself the chance to concentrate on the task before you fully.

- **Take Frequent Breaks**

Breaks are necessary as you go throughout your day. When you give yourself a break, you'll see your focus your concentration is improving because long runs of work without a break will "thin" your focus. Schedule breaks where you can think of something else entirely, you can leave your workspace, and give your brain a "breather." If you get caught up in your work, losing track of time, set a timer and alarm to remind it's time for a break. Remember: a five-minute break will rest your mind

- **Be Mindful of Your Physical Health**

Your physical health can affect your focus and concentration, as well. Take care of your body through proper nutrition, exercise, and minimal stress. Your body needs to be taken care of, or else everything that you work for will mean nothing. Never underestimate how valuable it is to maintain your physical well-being.

- **Remove Notifications**

Turn off notifications on your phone and all other devices. Every time you hear that ding, you are going to be tempted to check –

breaking your current train of thought. If you can't turn off your device, at least turn off the notifications.

- **Complete Your Dreaded Tasks First**

We all have tasks we dread and as hard as this is to hear: you need to tackle that dreaded task at the beginning of your day. Don't schedule it for later, because you'll spend your day with the task niggling at the back of your mind! By completing the task right away in the morning, you free your mind up in your focus to joyfully look towards everything else that you need to accomplish.

- **Eliminate Negative People from Your Life**

Negativity is another aspect of life that is going to attack your focus, your time, and your energy. Allowing negative people to dwell in your life will drain your ability to focus, and you will be constantly dragged down by the negative energy. Do not feel guilty for releasing negative relationships; your well-being needs to be a priority. Negativity has both mental and physical repercussions, and it doesn't matter if these toxic relationships are with family, friends, or co-workers – surrounding yourself with people who refuse to be positive is going to harm you. Set your sights on your goals and release any negativity in your life.

Practicing your focus and concentration is important to your success but remember the steps above and make them part of your daily routine. Invest your time in yourself and watch your focus and concentration skyrocket!

Chapter 7

Your self-esteem is a vital part of who you are, revealing how you feel about yourself and the confidence that you possess. Low self-esteem has many causes, and the goal should be to raise your self-esteem to a healthy level.

What Causes Low Self-Esteem?

Several reasons can be cited for low self-esteem. These reasons can be specific to children, adolescents, or adults. Let's look at the reasons for low self-esteem and else.

- **An Unhappy Childhood**

Adults who (as children) had caregivers who were either not involved, too involved, or too critical can experience low self-esteem later in life. Growing up being bullied or mistreated makes an individual feel unworthy. An unhappy childhood can cause you to feel like you are incapable of accomplishing your goals.

- **Mental Illness**

Certain mental illnesses, such as bipolar, depression, or anxiety, can cause you to have low self-esteem. Often these conditions are caused by a chemical imbalance in your brain or your situational condition. It's important to seek help if you feel that you have any issues with your mental health. It's also important to understand that mental illness is not something to be ashamed of, and often has little or nothing to do with anything that you've done wrong. If your self-esteem is suffering because of mental illness, know that you are not alone, and that assistance may be a phone call away.

- **Financial Troubles**

Having issues with your financial situation can be a major blow to your self-esteem. When your finances are in trouble, the situation can lead you to blame yourself. Often financial trouble has nothing to do with anything that you've done wrong, but as something to do with external factors. When external factors are responsible, blaming yourself serves no purpose. Your self-esteem can suffer when you allow your inner critic to get the best of you and blame you for your financial situation. Before you take the blame on yourself, take time to sort through your finances, and see where the issue arose.

- **Ongoing Medical Problems**

Your physical health can cause you to have low self-esteem. If you suffer from medical issues, often you are not able to do the things that you want to do, which in turn can cause you to feel poorly about yourself. Taking care of your physical health should be a priority, but sometimes no matter what you do, you still wind up with medical issues. Remember that you cannot control everything in life.

- **Poor Treatment by Partner or Others**

Abusive situations (verbal, emotional, or physical) clearly leads to poor self-esteem. It is important to get out of the situation as soon as possible and stop enabling the abusers. In an abusive situation, the abuser is the person who has problems, not the person being abused.

- **Being Bullied**

If you are a victim of bullying, your self-esteem will be affected. Bullying causes the individual to feel unworthy and inadequate. If you are the victim of bullying, either now or in the past, it's important to talk to someone about the way you are feeling. It's important to remember that you did nothing to cause the bullying, but the important idea to remember is to seek help so that you can be on the path to rediscovering how great you are.

- **Previous Academic Challenges**

An individual who struggled academically in school is also at risk for low self-esteem. It's often hard to remember that people learn differently, and as a result, an individual can suffer if they do not keep up with their peers academically.

- **Trauma**

Like victims of abuse, victims of trauma often feel like they have done something to deserve the experience. If you have suffered a traumatic event, consider seeking help to determine how the drama is affecting you, and how to move beyond it.

- **Societal and Media Pressure**

Media creates unrealistic images of both women and men: perfect bodies, beautiful/handsome faces, the latest and best clothing, sparkling white teeth. It's no wonder that this nonviable, unfeasible portrayal of men and women in our society leads to unrealistic expectations of what our bodies, minds, and personalities need to be. Remember that those are paid models, airbrushed, and photoshopped into that myth called "perfection."

How to Boost Your Self-Confidence and Quit Sabotaging Your Life

It's common that when your self-esteem is low, and you feel poorly about yourself, you may try sabotaging anything good that happens to you. This is a common occurrence because when you feel poorly about yourself, you feel that you do not deserve goodness and happiness. To overcome these feelings and to quit sabotaging your life, consider the tips below.

- **Learn a New Skill and Master It**

Nothing says that you are competent and worthy more than learning a new skill. You have the ability to learn something new and conquer that skill. Once mastered, your self-esteem should improve, bringing feelings of validation back to you.

- **Keep a Record of Your Accomplishments**

In your journal, keep a list of everything that you've been successful at. It doesn't matter how small the task may be, write it down. When you suffer low self-esteem, it helps to remember each small detail of everything that you have done wonderfully. Stop seeking validation from others and reflect upon the accomplishments that you have made in your lifetime.

- **Be Creative**

Creativity sparks self-love. Find a way to create something. Write a poem, draw a picture, paint, or work with raw materials to create something beautiful. Creativity is wonderful because you have the power to create something from nothing! Unharness your inventive and artistic side!

- **Define Your Values**

By defining what you believe in and living by those values, you are showing who you are as a person. If you believe in love and peace, look for ways to express those values to others. Your self-esteem will improve because when you live what you believe, you have a greater chance of succeeding. Remember that embracing who you are and living the life that you want is a wonderful way to be your own person.

- **Challenge the Limiting Beliefs That You Have**

Limiting beliefs are ones that tell you cannot do something because of a trait that you have, or a skill you are missing. Examples of limiting beliefs might be: "I can't do that, I'm a woman." Why not? Women fly airplanes, repair computers, solve mysteries, save lives, and teach others how to do the same! Believing that you are limited to what you can accomplish is going to cause you to feel poorly about yourself. Releasing these beliefs and embracing true beliefs about yourself is going to affect your self-esteem positively.

- **Get Out of Your Comfort Zone**

Are you stuck in a rut? Are you living each day the same as the one before? Chances are you're going to feel bad about yourself if you remain in your comfort zone. Being where you are comfortable is good to a certain extent, but if you never venture out of that zone, you run the risk of being complacent. Taking risks allows you to grow and learn as a person, and as a result, you are going to feel better about yourself for each accomplishment.

- **Come to Terms with Your Past**

The past is behind you, and there's nothing you can do to change it. Understanding this is going to allow you to come to terms with past events and choices. Once you understand and come to terms with the choices that you've made, you are going to feel freedom. Keeping yourself bogged down by memories of poor choices serves no purpose other than to hold you back from progress. Reflect upon the past, come to terms with it, and release it. Once you do this, you have the freedom to become who you are meant to be and to accomplish great things.

- **Stop Caring What Others Think**

Carrying the burden of trying to live up to somebody else's expectations is going to hold you back. No one should be required to live a life on someone else's terms because everyone is different. Walk away from that trap; others' opinions about you and your life are just that: Their opinions. Releasing yourself from concerns about their opinions allows you to feel freedom like you never have before.

- **Integrity**

Live your life with integrity. This means to hold yourself to a high moral standard and make sure that your life reflects that. When you practice integrity, you are showing the world that you are worthwhile, that you value yourself, and that you value others.

- **Release Negative Relationships**

Negative relationships hold you back. They also affect your self-esteem, and they can keep you from reaching your true potential. Relationships that cause you mental, physical, and emotional stress and harm should be released permanently. Do not cling to those in your life who do not value you and treat you with respect. You deserve more, and once you demand that, you're going to see your self-esteem improve.

- **Value Your Appearance**

When you put a value on your outward appearance, you show the world that you care about yourself. This does not mean being in the height of fashion, but rather, it means being properly groomed, clean, and neat. Taking care of how you look is going to make you feel better about yourself and show the world that you value who you are.

- **Embrace Failure and Grow from It**

Everyone fails at some point in life; those who say otherwise are likely lying. Failure is nothing more than an opportunity to learn and grow. Each time you feel like you failed at something, look for the learning opportunity. Embrace these opportunities and valuable life lessons. When you do that, and you reframe your negative thoughts about failure, you are going to feel better about yourself. By growing as an individual, you understand that you have the ability to move on and be greater when you were before.

- **Continue to Learn**

Just like mastering a new skill, learning continually boosts your self-esteem. Each new fact or tidbit that you learn is expanding your mind and growing you as an individual. Take pride in this! Not everyone makes it a practice to continue learning past traditional schooling. Expanding your mind is a good way to improve your self-esteem.

- **Embrace Your Fears**

Living life in a fearful state is no way to live. By embracing your fears and learning to act regardless of them, you are showing the world that you are resilient and strong. When you embrace your fears, you are going to feel better about yourself as you realize that nothing can hold you back.

- **Define Success for You**

Success looks different for each individual. Take the time to clearly define what success is going to look like for you. From there, reach for that success by setting goals that will help you along the journey, finding the determination to achieve each one of them. As you check the goals off your list, feel your self-esteem improve because you know that nothing is holding you back.

Understanding Who You Are

Self-awareness is vital to your success and will affect your mindset. It is also vital to understand who you are so that you can improve your self-esteem and maintain how you feel about yourself.

- **Embrace Your Feelings**

Feelings, whether they are positive or negative, affect who we are. Embrace every feeling and emotion that you have. We are taught from an early age that we need to hide or negative emotions, but this was a lie. Negative emotions have a place for expression in our lives, but we need to make sure that we are doing this appropriately. Use your positive and your negative emotions to your advantage and harness the energy that they produce. These emotions can drive you to be a better person and achieve your goals.

- **Seek Out Feedback**

Feedback is a great way for us to grow as individuals. Ask your boss, your coworkers, or your partner how you can improve. Remember, though: this is feedback, and this feedback is based on opinions. You need to compare the opinions of others to the facts that you know about yourself before making any changes.

- **Understand Your Strengths and Weaknesses**

We talked about understanding what your weaknesses are so that you can improve, but it's just important for you to understand what your strengths are as well. Knowing who you are, what you're good at, and where you need improvement is important to your self-esteem. Understand what you are good at so that you can take pride in those activities and tasks, but don't forget about areas needing improvement! Addressing each of those areas is going to boost your self-esteem.

- **Be Mindful**

Practicing mindfulness requires that you remain in the moment. Do not allow your mind to wander to past decisions or to worry about the future. Be mindful of who you are, where you are at in life, and where you are going. Everything else does not require your attention at the moment. When you focus on who you are right now, your self-esteem is going to improve because you can see that you are working towards your success.

- **Remain Open-Minded**

It's important to keep an open mind about new ideas, people, and places. Being open-minded is going to ensure that you are looking at different perspectives which - in turn – helps you avoid becoming judgmental. When you are open-minded, this benefits your self-esteem because you are making better choices.

Visualization

Visualization is an effective technique that allows you to see the results and experience them before they happen. There are several tips and techniques that you can use to practice visualization. Below you will find some effective strategies for making visualization part of your life.

- **Use Affirmations and Expect Results**

Affirmations are highly effective statements that allow you to trigger positive feelings within your mind., activating the Law of Attraction. These positive statements proclaim what you expect every day: I will succeed. I am worthwhile. I will reach my goals.

- **Index Cards**

Use index cards to record each goal you have, keeping them near your bed and going through them one at a time. With each visualization, spend 15 seconds imagining the result of these goals. Make sure that you are doing this regularly until your goals are achieved.

- **Create Goal Pictures**

Goal pictures are a photo or up drawing showing yourself reaping the benefits of reaching your goals. Study these, imagine that you are there, your goal achieved! You can draw yourself in a drawing, or you can use Photoshop to put yourself into the photo. Some examples would be taking a picture of yourself at a car dealership behind the wheel of your dream car and photoshopping yourself into an office space that the picture exactly what you want. This is an effective way to see exactly what you want your life to look like.

- **For Each Picture Attached in Affirmation**

Each photo or picture that you have depicting yourself achieving your goals should have an affirmation attached to it. This is effective because when you repeat that affirmation, it will not matter if you have the pictures in front of you are not because the affirmation is going to bring that goal to mind. The benefits of visualizing yourself completing your goals are numerous.

- **Activating Creativity**

When you use visualization, you are allowing yourself to take a creative approach to complete your goals. Visualization requires you to use your imagination.

- **Programs Your Brain to Recognize What You Need to Achieve Your Dreams**

Visualization is an exercise that trains your brain to recognize what you need (or need to do) to achieve your dreams. Think of this as an exercise where you are building the willpower and the stamina needed to complete a goal. As you visualize, you are looking at each step that needs to be taken so that you can accomplish this in real life.

- **Activates the Law of Attraction**

Remember that the Law of Attraction means that you are manifesting whatever it is you desire from life. You can manifest money, thoughts, actions, and more. The universe will give you what you desire if you practice a positive mindset.

- **Builds Internal Motivation**

Being internally motivated is important. When you rely on factors outside of yourself for motivation, you're going to be disappointed. Recognition, awards, and bonuses are nice, but learn to rely on your internal motivation to serve you well throughout your lifetime as you pursue your goals. The satisfaction that you get from achieving your goals should be enough.

Your self-esteem is important to who you are and how you achieve your goals. You need to make sure that you are taking care of yourself and doing everything you can to boost your self-esteem. View yourself as worthy, important, and deserving of the best life has to offer!

Chapter 8:
Mental Toughness

Being mentally tough means that you can withstand constructive criticism, disappointment, and failure. Mental toughness keeps you going when the going gets rough; you can continue pursuing your goals despite the setbacks you experience.

Characteristics of Mentally Tough Individuals

Perhaps you will surprise yourself and find that you already have the characteristics of somebody who is mentally tough. On the other hand, you could learn new ways that are going to benefit you throughout your lifetime.

- **Confidence**

When you believe in yourself, you have one of the basic characteristics of mental toughness. You understand that you will succeed because of who you are, the abilities (natural or obtained) that you have, and because you have self-confidence. Confidence is vital to mental toughness because you need to believe that you *can* succeed in order *to* succeed.

- **Confident in Challenges**

A person with mental toughness understands that to grow continually, one needs to be willing to learn from the challenges that are set before him. He/she understandings that focusing on achieving positive outcomes leads to success. By understanding that challenges are necessary to grow, your idea of "success" may change. While "success" looks different to everybody, a mentally tough individual realizes that part of success involves learning from the obstacles being faced.

- **Control**

Mentally tough individuals understand that the power to shape their destiny lies within them; they control their lives and their destiny - life does not control them. They have full confidence in the control they possess in terms of their life's success, and they bask in this knowledge.

- **Commitment**

The commitment of an individual with mental toughness is insurmountable. They understand that setting goals is an important step, and that facing adversity head-on makes then the victor. There is no reason to shy away from challenges or adversity when you are committed to doing what you need to do to achieve your goals.

Practicing Mental Toughness

Perhaps at this point time, you are wondering how to practice and improve mental toughness. Read the tips below and set yourself up for success!

- **Set Goals**

You've heard this in previous chapters; make a commitment by setting goals. This messages the universe that you are willing to do what it takes to be successful. You know what you want out of life, and you are going to create that no matter how hard the path may be.

- **Set Yourself Up for Success**

How do you go about setting yourself up for success? It's not complicated! To be successful, you need to learn, you need to seek feedback for improvement, you need to understand how to reshape your thought processes, and you need to be willing to make changes as necessary. By now, I'm sure you have already begun the process of setting yourself up for success. If you haven't, now is the perfect time to begin.

- **Embrace Discomfort for the Greater Good**

Growing hurts. It doesn't matter if it's something that you want, growing as an individual is going to be uncomfortable. You must face realities about yourself that you may not be fully prepared to consider. Even if this is the case, you understand that improvement begins with the discomfort of knowing you need to grow. Embrace this discomfort and know that it is going to lead to something better.

- **Reframe Your Negative Thought Processes**

As we discussed, negativity serves no purpose in your life other than to hold you back. Learn to reframe negative thought processes by stopping negative thoughts in their tracks. When you experience a negative thought, make a conscious effort to switch that negative thought into a positive one. The more you practice this, the easier it gets!

- **Balance Out Your Emotions with Logic**

Logic needs to win out above your emotions. Emotions are volatile and can often lead you down the wrong path. Each time you feel yourself getting highly emotional, make a conscious effort to slow down and let logic kick in. As you practice this, it becomes second nature to reign in your emotions, living life with a logical approach, not fleeting emotions.

- **Fulfill Your Purpose**

You need to figure out what you are meant to do. Are you meant to be a writer? Perhaps you are meant to lead a successful business? You need to take the time to determine your purpose(s) in life so that you can get busy *being* the person you are meant to be. Life will not have meaning until you live to your true potential.

- **Explanations, Not Excuses**

Mentally tough individuals do not deal with excuses. They may have explanations for why they failed or why they succeeded, but these are not to be confused with excuses. Excuses place blame and explanations accept responsibility. Individuals who display mental toughness understand that they need to accept responsibility for their actions and their choices, whether it leads to success or failure.

- **<u>Try One Hard Task Daily</u>**

You cannot be a wimp if you hope to succeed. You need to try hard tasks, or else you are not challenging yourself. Mentally tough individuals understand that a challenge is a way for them to grow. Each day, strive to be successful at one task that you find hard for you, sticking with it for at least ten minutes. In these ten minutes, give yourself a pep talk, boosting your motivation and building momentum to finish. Mentally tough individuals understand that finishing is important, and success is not necessarily important.

- **<u>Take Satisfaction in Proving Yourself Wrong</u>**

When you doubt yourself, enjoy the moment when you are proven wrong. It's no fun to be proven wrong by somebody else but take great satisfaction when you prove yourself wrong! Being wrong means that you are capable of more than you think you are. Mentally strong individuals embrace their strengths and their weaknesses because they know that both are going to play to their advantage and are important to their success.

<u>Developing Positive Habits</u>

To develop mental toughness, you need first to begin developing positive habits. Mentally tough individuals understand that positive habits are going to take them far in life. They work hard to develop these habits and incorporate them into their daily routine.

- **<u>Act as If You Are in Control</u>**

Even when you are not in control, you must act as if you are! When life feels like it is spiraling out of control, it is important to maintain the façade that you are in control and life is not. As the phrase goes: "Fake it 'til you make it!" This is important when you are dealing with control. Believe that you have control of your life and your situation even when you feel completely useless. The control will come in time but pretending that you have it is going to give you the confidence to proceed until you are once again in control.

- **Discard What You Have No Control Over**

There is no point in holding onto something that is out of your control; you are only hurting yourself. Time and energy are going to be wasted on a situation, task, or projects that you have no control over. Make sure that you identify early on if something is within your control or not, and you will see your outcomes change from negative to positive.

- **The Past can Provide Valuable Training**

Your past is nothing but a series of lessons that you learn from life. Do not dwell on the past but rather take the life lessons and treat them as a training exercise. Learning to be objective about your past helps you see the valuable training that you had within you all along. Remember that each failure or disappointment is nothing more than a learning exercise and does not reflect on you as a person.

- **Celebrate Others Success**

Mentally tough individuals understand the importance of celebrating the success of other people. By celebrating the success of other individuals, you understand that their success plays no part in yours. Celebrate each accomplishment that people in your life achieve because when you achieve your success, those same individuals are going to be there cheering you on. Remember that others succeeding does not mean you are going to fail.

- **Stop Complaining, Whining, and Criticizing**

Complaining means that you're not willing to do the work to achieve the outcome that you want. Whining shows that you are not accepting responsibility for your part. Criticizing only serves the purpose of making you appear less grateful and bitter about other people's success. Complaining, whining, and criticizing is only going to bring you down, turning your mindset negative. Remember the importance of a positive mindset as you are trying to fulfill your goals.

- **Impress Only Yourself**

You do not need to impress other individuals in life. The only person that you should set out to impress is yourself because your opinion matters - other people's opinions don't. When you set out to impress only yourself, you are going to find that you are more satisfied in life and that your success is that much sweeter. Mentally strong individuals understand that the opinions of others do not matter, taking those opinions with a grain of salt, comparing them to the facts they know about themselves and their lives. If they find themselves coming up short, they know that all they can do is strive to improve.

- **Count Your Blessings**

Being grateful is an important part of achieving your dreams. Practicing a grateful attitude shows others the importance of knowing exactly where you are in life. The blessings that you have been given help in driving you towards success; grateful people understand the importance of hard work and discipline.

- **Develop Emotional Intelligence**

Emotional intelligence involves using your own emotions to your advantage, understanding the emotions of others and basing your actions on that understanding. Emotional intelligence is important as a skill because when you can relate better to the emotions that other people are feeling, your interpersonal relationships are going to improve. A large part of emotional intelligence is empathy. Empathy requires that you look at different perspectives and try to view life from another person's point of view.

- **Say No**

Learning to say no is another valuable tool in your arsenal. Saying "no" is not rude, and you are not showing less care for other people. In reality, you are showing other people that you value your time and your energy. By saying no, you are staying true to your values, and you are living life according to those values. Be sure to give a reason when you say "no" so that others' understand you have a valid reason. Refuse to do activities or take on tasks that do not align with your goals or your values.

- **Fear is the Only Reason to Regret**

The only reason that you should regret a past decision is if it was driven by fear. Remember that you need to overcome your fears to succeed.

- **Embrace Failure and Let Go of Mistakes**

Failure is an opportunity to learn, and when you realize that you are going to see that your mindset changes. Mentally strong individuals understand the importance of embracing their failure in releasing past mistakes. Mistakes provide a pathway to learning. Think of when you are learning to walk or ride a bike. When you fell, did you give up, or did you continue to try? If you gave up chances are you would not be reading this book. I'm going to go out on a limb and say that you continued to try. You probably did not realize that when you were learning to ride a bike, each time you fell you were making mental assessments of what went wrong *that* time! Life is similar; when you learn from your mistakes, you will find that it is easier to let them go.

- **Forgive**

To be successful and healthy as an individual, you need to practice forgiveness. Forgiveness is important to extend to others who may have wronged you or made poor choices that affected you. This is also important for you to practice with yourself. Make sure that when you slip up or you make a mistake that you are forgiving yourself and moving on.

- **Remain Positive**

Positivity can be hard to maintain unless you are mentally strong. Mental toughness allows you to keep a positive attitude even when you feel like the world is falling around you. Try to keep an optimistic view of life, your goals, and your relationships. This is going to allow you to be more successful and achieve your dreams.

Advantages to Mental Strength

Being mentally tough has its advantages, and below you'll find a few (in case you need to be convinced to develop this skill!)

- **Develops Leadership Skills**

Later in the book, we are going to talk about leadership and how being mentally tough is related. Leadership skills required that you can take criticism, feedback, and tough situations without crumbling. Mental toughness allows you to remain a positive leader despite the circumstances around you.

- **Conquers Doubt**

Doubting yourself is not going to serve any purpose when setting out to achieve goals and be successful in life. With a positive mindset and mental toughness, you can quiet the doubt that you may be feeling and instead embrace the positive success that is coming your way.

- **Develop and Maintain Motivation**

Mental toughness gives you the ability to switch from being externally motivated to being internally motivated. Internal motivation is something you drive; external motivation is being driven by someone else. When you rely on external factors to drive you to be successful, you are going to be disappointed. Learning mental toughness is going to allow you to develop an internal motivation which will help you on your journey to conquering your goals.

- **Unhelpful Advice**

Unhelpful feedback serves no purpose other than squashing your spirit. Mental toughness allows you to filter out the unhelpful advice and keep only the helpful recommendations that come your way.

- **Helps You Learn from Your Mistakes**

Being mentally tough is going to allow you to take the lessons from your mistakes and apply them to your life. When you get a handle on this, remember learning from your mistakes allows you to release them. There's no reason to dwell on mistakes other than to learn the lesson and let them go.

- **Gives You the Courage to Face Your Fears**

Mentally tough individuals understand that facing their fears is the only way that they can proceed forward. Make sure that you understand how important it is to treat fear as a motivator and not as a hindrance. To be successful, you need to take the energy from your fear and apply it to the situation. When you can learn to do that, you will have achieved a certain level of mental toughness that is going to see you being successful throughout your life.

Being mentally tough is vital to your life because, without it, you are going to struggle to accomplish your goals. Adopting the right mindset and learning how to remain mentally strong will help you in your relationships, in life, and in your career.

Chapter 9

Your social skills are something that you need to continually develop throughout your lifetime. Without effective social skills, you are going to struggle in your relationships, in your career, and in life in general. Understanding how to become socially intelligent is an important part of growing.

Communication: The Backbone of Relationships

Some people enjoy communicating, and others find it tiresome. No matter which person you are, it is important that you develop your communication skills so that you can be an effective person in life.

- **Make It a Priority**

Your communicating style needs your scrutiny! Once you have determined how you communicate best, make it a priority to hone the skills and leave the flaws behind. Increase your vocabulary, practice your written message, and work on your speaking skills. By making communication a priority, you are going to learn how to best engage other individuals.

- **Simplify Your Message and Stay on Track**

Verbally rattling on and on about your message or becoming sidetracked and telling random stories is not effective communication. When somebody's listening to you, it is courteous to be sure you clear, concise, and stay on point. Remember that unless the message is delivered effectively, it will lose its meaning.

- **Engage Your Listeners**

Asking questions and allowing the people who are listening to you to respond is a good way to keep them engaged in what you're saying. Remember how important it is to keep people engaged in your message; if you forget to keep them interested, your message is going to get lost. When you set out to communicate with someone, it's important to make sure that you are respectful to their needs as well.

- **Respond to Them**

Speaking of being respectful to your audience's needs, it's important that you respond to questions, comments, and body language. Notice if they seem uncomfortable or uninterested, changing directions and re-engaging them as necessary. When you are responsive to your audience, you'll find they are more responsive to you as well.

- **Make Sure You Are Understood**

Avoid being vague, or you risk the chance that you will be misunderstood. If your topic happens to be a delicate one, it is more important than ever that you ensure that your audience understands what you're trying to convey. Avoid off-color jokes, and keep the message audience-appropriate.

- **Develop Listening Skills**

As you are learning to communicate with others, it's important that you also learn how to listen. Active listening involves making sure that your mind does not wander, ensuring that you are receiving the appropriate message, and maintaining eye contact with the speaker. Active listening is going to serve you well throughout your lifetime, so consider honing this skill as soon as possible.

- **Use Appropriate Body Language**

Body language is important. When you are communicating with others, it's important to be mindful of not only the audience's body language but your body language as well. Standing with your arms crossed, for example, indicates that you are either angry, bored, or disinterested. Rolling your eyes is a sign of disrespect and gives the indication that you do not agree, or you want to disengage from the conversation. Make sure your body language matches the tone of your voice, being mindful of your facial expressions as well. Smiling during a sad story is inappropriate. Ber mindful to display proper emotions and be willing to work on your body language during communication.

- **Maintain Eye Contact**

Making or maintaining eye contact can be affected by the individual's background. Some cultures find it rude to maintain eye contact with the speaker. In American culture, it is considered rude not to maintain eye contact when somebody is speaking. Eye contact seen as a way to show that you are engaged in your listening. Based on your cultural preferences, try to maintain eye contact with the speaker to show that you are listening, and you are engaged in what they are saying.

What Was Your Name? Tips to Remember Names

Do you have a hard time remembering names? I do! If you struggle with remembering names, especially right after they were given to you, this section is for you. Below you will find some tips to help you remember and improve your social intelligence.

- **Make the Commitment to Remember Names**

You must make a commitment to strengthening your name-recalling skills, going the extra mile, using all the resources available to you. This commitment to remember names shows that you value relationships - even the new ones that you have just made.

- **Concentrate and Focus on The Person You Are Speaking To**

This is especially important when you are meeting new individuals. When you are in a conversation with someone else, it's important that you maintain focus and you concentrate on what the person is saying. This becomes vital when engaging with someone that you do not know. Make an effort to remain mindful during a conversation. This is going to help you link the name and the conversation that you had with the individual.

- **Repeat the Person's Name**

This is a tip that it seems everybody has heard. When you say hello, it is important to repeat the person's name: "Hello, John. Nice to meet you!" This habit helps solidify the name in your mind.

- **Make an Association Between the Name and The Person**

Associating somebody's name with a trait that they have is another good way to remember. Try to find a link between the name and the person's face, for example: "Cass with the glasses." How you associate the face with the name is up to you but find a trick that's going to help you remember his or her name.

- **Don't Have Another Conversation in Your Head**

This goes along with focusing and concentrating on the person that is speaking. When you focus on what the other person is saying, you cannot have another conversation in your head. Additionally, this keeps you from rehearsing your response while the other person is still speaking. Be courteous and remain mindful and at the moment when another person is speaking. This is going to ensure that you are able to remember their name because you are more likely to remember the conversation.

- **Repeat the Name When You Say Goodbye**

We already discussed repeating the name right after you meet the individual. It's also important to repeat the name as you tell them goodbye – just another step towards cementing their name in your ind. It's also helpful to repeat the person's name during the conversation but try not to make it awkward. It's also perfectly acceptable to repeat the name a few times and make a joke about how you are horrible with names. This helps break the ice, and it also helps the other person understand that you value them because you are trying to remember their name.

- **Review New Names at The End of The Day**

If you are in the business of meeting new people on a continual basis, a good practice to adopt is reviewing new names at the end of the day. Picture the name and the person and keep that association strong. The likelihood that you will remember them later one grows each time you are able to link their name to their face.

Improve Your Presentation Skills

To be an effective presenter, you need to practice. Plan out your presentation and make a point to practice more than twice. Practice in front of the mirror, practice in front of other people, record yourself practicing, and then view the results. As you look at yourself during the presentation, make notes, pay attention to your body language, and work on your expressions. The practice is vital to making your presentation flawless and effective.

- **Transform Nervous Energy into Enthusiasm**

Do you struggle with public speaking? If so, you understand what nervous energy is. Ignore the nervous part of that energy and transform it into enthusiasm. It's important that you appear enthusiastic even if you have butterflies floating around inside you. The most effective way to do that is to pretend that you are as enthusiastic as you would like your audience to view you.

- **Watch Other Presenters**

If you're presenting at a conference, watch other presentations, gauging the reaction of the audience and tweaking your own presentation based on those observations. If you don't have the opportunity to view other speakers in person, watch Ted talks or how-to videos on YouTube. Note and incorporate into your own presentation the positive habits of speakers, also taking note of any negative tendencies you can avoid in your own presentation.

- **Arrive Early**

Make an appointment arrived early to assess the environment around you, greeting people as they enter, making sure to engage a few of them. Arriving early allows you to look at your surroundings and calmly begin your presentation without feeling rushed.

- **Smile**

Smiling is the most important thing that you can do when you're presenting. By smiling, you're giving yourself a chance to feel as confident as you are trying to portray. A smile causes you to relax and connects you with your audience.

- **Use Positive Visualization**

We have discussed how important visualization is, and when you use positive visualization to gauge and determine how your presentation is going to go, you've just upped your success rate. It's important to visualize what could go wrong and try to envision how you would react to that. As you're going through your speech, visualizing how the audience is going to respond, it's important that you are also adding in some setbacks or obstacles that could potentially interrupt your presentation. Envision how you're going to react, and this is going to help you already have a pattern in your mind about what could go wrong and what could go right. Knowing how you would react in different situations is a good way to prepare yourself and to calm yourself beforehand.

- **Remember to Breathe Deeply**

Breathing deeply is an effective way to calm yourself down. Before you start your presentation, make sure that you are taking a few deep breaths so that you give yourself a chance to get acclimated to your surroundings. If during your speech you begin to feel nervous or you get jittery, take a moment to pause. An effective and well-timed pause gives the appearance of confidence when, in reality, you are just giving yourself a chance to catch up.

- **Don't Cover Too Much Material**

When covering how to improve your social skills, I mentioned the importance of simplifying your message and staying on track. This applies to presentations as well. Be specific in what you're talking about, and do not cover too much material or you may bore your audience. Your objective in giving a presentation is to deliver information in an engaging manner so that the people can learn as much as they can without falling asleep!

- **Work on Pausing**

Pauses can be an effective part of presentations. By inserting pauses appropriately, you not only provide an opportunity to gather your thoughts, you are giving the audience a chance to digest your message. When practicing your presentation, consider optimal places you can incorporate effective pauses.

- **Encourage Audience Interaction**

As you begin your speech, encourage interaction with your audience. This helps them understand your message and gives you a chance to see if you need to change direction in delivery. Encourage questions and comments as a way to keep your audience from zoning out.

- **Be Entertaining**

No one likes to sit through a presentation with a person who speaks in a monotone, delivering dull fact after dull fact. Toss in some personal stories, jokes, or other lighthearted material that allows your audience to take a mental break while you are speaking.

- **Admit That You Don't Know Everything**

No one has all the answers, so admit that in the beginning of your presentation. Your humility assures the audience that while you know quite a bit on the topic, you do not expect them to believe you know everything.

- **Use A Powerful Stance**

This tip is handy *before you go up on stage.* Stand in the Superman pose, putting your hands on your hips, sticking your chest out, and looking upwards with confidence. Practice the stance for 30 seconds before you go in front of your audience, and you will find that you feel more confident as you go forward.

- **Drink Water**

Hydration is important, especially when giving a presentation. Do not be afraid to take a glass or water bottle with you on stage; it may give you a moment to pause, gather your thoughts, and reassess your approach, if necessary. If you are speaking for a long time, it's very important to remain hydrated so that you don't feel faint or sick throughout your presentation. That said, don't overdo it or you may find yourself needing to take an unexpected bathroom break!

- **Embrace the Fear**

Do you have a fear of public speaking? Many people do, and the problem with that is that you doubt your own competence. The chances are that you would not have been asked to speak if other people did not view you as an expert in your field. Transform that fear into confidence by accepting the fact that others see you as competent in your field. Recite that to yourself before you go on stage and use affirmations to ensure success.

The Art of Constructive Feedback

If you are in a position of leadership, constructive feedback is vital to that role. Even if you're not in the position of leadership, understanding constructive feedback is going to serve you in your relationships.

• **Focus on The Problem and Be Specific**

If you are giving constructive feedback, chances are you are giving this feedback in relation to a problem or an or an issue that needs to be addressed. Make sure that you focus on the problem, staying specific in terms of why this is a problem; this is no time to be vague.

• **Discuss the Situation – not the Individual**

Effective feedback concentrates on the situation or the problem that needs to be addressed. Do not make this about the person you are speaking to, running the risk of ruining the feedback you intent to provide. Discussing the situation allows the person to see what was done wrong, instead of centering on how they were wrong. Focus on the problem, not the person.

• **Give Praise When Needed**

It is vital that you praise the individual when the situation calls for it. Even if you are in the position of having to use feedback to correct the situation, find a way to give praise, boosting their confidence, solidifying your relationship, and ensuring that the feedback is received properly.

• **Be Direct, but Keep an Informal Attitude**

Formality and stiffness can hinder feedback reception. Address the situation directly but do so in an informal way. An example: rather than meeting in a formal office or conference room, sit across from the individual without any obstruction between you. This allows you to appear more informal and gives the illusion that you and the individual are merely having a conversation. Make sure that when you are delivering feedback that you are sitting and relaxed. Be mindful of your body language and ensure that you are not delivering the wrong message. Your words and your body language need to match up.

- **Be Sincere**

People can pick up on insincerity. No one enjoys being spoken to and treated in a condescending manner. When you are insincere, you come across as condescending, and this can damage your relationship with the other individual. Make sure that what you say is what you mean, and make sure that your tone matches your words.

- **Listen**

Feedback is only constructive if you're listening to what the other individual is saying. Giving the other person the opportunity to speak and share their opinion reduces the chance of them feeling attacked.

- **Be Timely**

Do not wait too long to deliver constructive feedback. If the feedback is related to a specific incident, it's important that you address the incident quickly and not wait too long.

- **Focus on How to Change and Point Out Opportunities**

When giving constructive feedback, it's important that you focus on the change that needs to be made and the opportunities that the individual has to make these changes. When you focus on change in opportunity, your feedback is going to come across as positive and will be received better. By focusing on change and opportunities, you are ensuring that the individual is going to take your comments to heart, and actually look forward to the changes that they can make.

- **Prepare the Person for The Feedback**

When delivering feedback, it doesn't hurt to prepare the person. Using a phrase such as "you may not like what I have to say" or "This may be hard to hear, but it's necessary" can help prepare the individual for what may be difficult feedback. No matter how much you want them to receive the feedback positively, there is always a chance that the person will not see any positivity in your conversation. The person may believe that you are attacking them and close down emotionally. Remember to give some thought to how you might prepare the other person for this difficult conversation.

- **Make the Conversation Private**

Nobody likes to be corrected in public! Make sure that you are in an informal setting, but also that there is privacy. This allows the other person to focus on what you are saying and not who is listening. This is a respectful approach.

- **Begin by Pointing Out the Good**

Do not start out with negative feedback, but rather start out with the positive qualities of the individual. This opens the lines of communication which are going to be important throughout the conversation.

- **Maintain Communication**

After you've delivered your feedback, make sure that you keep the lines of communication open. Offer opportunities to state opinions – even if those opinions are in direct disagreement with your position. Giving the other person the option to speak ensures that even after the feedback is given, the lines of communication are going to remain open.

- **Discuss Action**

Let the individual know that there is an action that they can take, providing opportunities that are available to them. Empowering the other individual to take action on their own behalf is a good form of leadership. Leaders understand that empowerment is going to serve them better than tearing an individual down. Lay out steps to correct the situation and make them action oriented.

- **Remain Objective and Respectful**

Do not allow your personal feelings to enter into the conversation. Keep your perspective objective, respecting the person as an individual and understanding that their emotions and their needs play a part in that conversation. You are showing your skills as an effective leader when giving respect along with constructive feedback.

- **Use Your Emotional Intelligence**

This is vital because when you understand what the other person is feeling, you are able to act accordingly. Navigating their feelings as you provide feedback shows emotional intelligence! Before you begin the conversation, make sure that you have considered the other person's perspective.

Your social skills are going to determine the success of your relationships, the work that you do, and the opportunities that present themselves throughout your lifetime. Keep in mind that your social skills require a lifetime of commitment to practicing and improving them.

Chapter 10

Are you currently a leader in your profession? Perhaps you are someone who desires to be a leader? If so, this chapter is for you! We will discuss the different types of leadership, learn what your superpower is, and effective leadership skills you'll need to become successful. Here are some valuable tips on how to bravely embrace leadership.

Learning Your Superpower

Your superpower is simply something that you do well and with passion. Do you already know your superpower? Perhaps you are on a quest to find your superpower: read on. We are going to learn how to find the superpower within us and use that superpower to better our circumstances.

- **List What You Do Well**

The first step in discovering your superpower is understanding what it is that you do well. List everything that you do well, even if it is simply cleaning the toilet. Each task that you can perform to near perfection should be on this list. You should feel empowered by this list, your self-esteem should be boosted, and there should be nothing on this list that makes you feel bad about yourself.

- **What Comes Naturally?**

From that superpower list, which activities and tasks come naturally to you? Pick out each ability listed that you can do with your eyes closed. It's something that you just automatically know how to do without thinking. Create a separate list from the first one, considering each ability that you naturally possess. We will keep creating lists and eventually narrow them down until we discover your superpower!

- **What Are You Passionate About?**

On that second list, cross out everything that you are not passionate about. Anything on that list that doesn't set a fire burning in your soul – cross it off! Consider each option thoroughly because this is an important activity.

- **Which of These Items Makes Time Disappear?**

As you are thinking about your list, write down anything that you are able to do that makes time simply disappeared. What is something that you do where you can lose track of time entirely? This is an activity that you cannot start if you have another responsibility later. If you engage in this activity and have an appointment you must go to, you understand that you must set an alarm to break the focus and concentration required by this activity! For example, you might be painting, writing, giving a friend advice; whatever the activity, it comes naturally to you and you are deeply passionate about it.

- **What Makes You Different?**

This is an interesting way to understanding your superpower because now we need to look at what makes you slightly different - or perhaps a lot different - from your peers. Each of us has an ability that makes us just a little bit different than everybody else. There is a likelihood that more than one ability is going to come to mind. Ensure that you are paying attention and that you are taking your time to think these lists through. This is not something that you are going to accomplish in a day, but rather this is something that may take some time; that's fine. It's important to look at the different abilities, skills, and strengths that you have that are going to set you apart from the other people.

- **Consider Why Others Would Seek Advice from You**

Perhaps you are a skilled writer, and your friends and family often seek your advice when they must prepare a report, write a letter, or create a resume. Perhaps you have exceptional people skills, allowing you to easily read others' emotions, see their perspective, or anticipate how they are going to react to different situations. Think about time people asked for your advice: what were you giving advice on? List those things and proceed to the next step.

- **When You Were a Child, What Did You Love to Do?**

This one is a fun and exciting step. Think back to when you were a child all the way up through your teen years, considering what you enjoyed doing the most. It's a very interesting concept because what you enjoy doing as a child is going to translate into what you are going to do as an adult. Each activity that you had as a child is preparing you for adulthood. Consider if you enjoyed imaginative play. How is this going to translate into an adult skill? Perhaps this makes you a writer, this could make you an actress or an actor, or this could make you an effective presenter. Notice how one's skill can give you many different superpowers. Make a list of everything that you enjoyed doing as a child – leave nothing out!

- **If Money Was No Object…**

Take your time to consider what you would do with your life if you didn't have to worry about money? Would you begin a career speaking on topics that you are passionate about? Would you teach children or adults? Consider each activity or task that you would do if you didn't need a paycheck.

- **Look at The Answer That Is on Each List**

Some items are going to pop up on the different lists you have created. You may find yourself crossing off some items as they become less applicable. Consider how these skills are interrelated. Look at how you are able to use them in daily life. How do these translate into real-life situations?

Have you come up with your superpower from your list? This exercise is important because if you do not find the correlation between what you do well, what you enjoy doing, and what comes naturally to you, you are not going to discover your superpower. Look at the individual qualities, abilities, and skills that you have and make them translate into a real-life situation. Chances are you're going to have several options and these options are going to be crystal clear by the end of this activity. I wish you luck in finding your superpower, and I hope you find all the success in the world once you have discovered why you have this strange collection of skills and abilities.

Types of Leadership

There are six different types of leadership; determine which type of leader you are and apply that leadership type to the next few sections of the book. Once you figure out how to apply your leadership style to your life, you are going to see that success finds you.

- **Democratic Leadership**

The democratic leadership style invites participation from team members. When making decisions, the democratic leader is going to seek advice and opinions from team members and incorporate those into decision-making.

- **Autocratic Leadership**

This type of leadership style is an aggressive personality who seeks to the power to control everyone and everything involved, making decisions without consulting team members. These types of leaders often demand work and expect the results immediately. This is a very strong individual and their personality tends to be overpowering.

- **Coaching Leadership**

This is the most ideal and most effective type of leadership, allowing for empowerment rather than control. These leaders lead indirectly.

- **Strategic Leadership**

This leadership style is one that can influence the success of others and represents another type of empowering leadership.

- **Transformational Leadership**

This leader creates a thriving work environment, using effective communication and allowing team members to interject their opinions on important matters.

What's your leadership style? Is it effective? Read on to compare your leadership style to the effective leadership skills shown below.

Effective Leadership and The Skills That You Need

To lead effectively, you need to have a variety of skills in your arsenal so that you are able to make use of your team members and their abilities.

- **Have a Vision**

It's important that you know what you want, where you are going, and how you are going to get there. This is important in your personal life but it is also vital if you are leading others. Make sure that you communicate your vision with your team members, reminding them of this vision as you lead.

- **Lead by Example**

Do not expect people to follow the lead of someone who expects others to meet standards that he feels do not apply to himself. Become an example of the type of individual you want on your team. A leader is someone that empowers and inspires others to follow them. Consider how you lead: is it by example or is it "Do as I say, not as I do"?

- **Displaying Integrity**

Integrity means living and leading with a strong moral compass. If you are a leader, integrity is vital. Make sure that your life reflects the integrity that is within you. If it does not, consider making some changes. Effective leaders display integrity and they live their life as an example to others.

- **Effectively Communicate**

The chapter on communication was important your personal life but it is even more important if you are a leader. Learning how to communicate effectively is going to inspire change in your team members and it will empower them as well. Use all of the effective communication skills that you have in your toolkit and you will see success through your team members.

- **Make the Tough Calls**

Leaders can make calls that may be unpopular and that may result in criticism. As a leader, you need to be able to make these tough calls. Tough calls can include firing someone, adopting a policy that may be unpopular, or simply adopting a schedule that may leave others unhappy. You are a leader for a reason, and you need to lead by example. Your goal is to empower, not be popular.

- **Acknowledge Success**

As a leader, it is important for you to pay attention to successful results. You need to seek out the individuals that are consistently bringing in successful outcomes. This is going to endear your team members to you because they know that you appreciate the work that they are doing. As a leader, this is an important skill; your team members need to have confidence that you are seeing what is happening around you. As you acknowledge the success of those around you, you are going to see the outcomes of your team members improve.

- **Empower Others**

Empowering others is an important part of leadership. Give your team members the tools that they need to be successful. Empowering them involves setting them up for success, and then praising them when they achieve this. Think of leaders who have empowered you to be better and to move on in life.

- **Motivate and Inspire**

We have discussed the importance of internal motivation is, but when you are a leader it is your job to offer extra motivation. This can be in the form of acknowledgments, bonuses, or simply better tasks to complete. It never hurts to motivate your team members to improve and work harder. Oftentimes this happens when you offer some sort of external reward. Being inspirational is something that you need to work on because inspiring your team members is just as important as and motivating them. Give them a reason for successful outcomes and watch the environment around you change! An inspiring and motivating leader can change a work environment from poor to excellent with little effort. Strive to be that leader.

- **Persuasion and Influence**

How are you at using your influence to get results? Influence and persuasion simply mean that you can use your skills, abilities, and work effectively to make others do what you want them to do. Sometimes persuasion and influence are used in a negative way, but an effective leader is going to be able to use these for good outcomes.

- **People Management**

How well are you able to manage the human resources at your disposal? When you see each person as an individual, acknowledging their skills and abilities, you'll find that managing them becomes easier. Learning how to use the personalities of each team member to balance out quirks of another is going to serve you well over the long run. Consider how leaders in your life have balanced out the working environment by teaming up certain individuals to create successful outcomes.

Tips to Bravely Embrace Leadership

Do you find it scary when thinking about being a leader? The chances are if you are in the role of being a leader, whether it is at work or in your personal life, you are in this position for a reason. You have demonstrated the qualities and abilities of an effective leader and sought out to lead others. Below you will find tips that will help you embrace the scary quest of leadership.

- **Realize Your Leadership Gift**

You more than likely have an innate gift for leadership. Look at your strengths that align with the above-mentioned skills of effective leaders. How do these intertwine? Consider your personality, your skills, your abilities, and your way with people. Embrace the gifts that you have within you to effectively lead others to successful outcomes.

- **Immerse Yourself in Learning and Growth Opportunities**

Remember that learning is a continual activity and this is no different when you are learning to be an effective leader. If you are willing to continue improving and growing, you'll find that others seeks you out to lead. Never stop learning because new ideas and concepts are discovered constantly. When you are leading individuals, understanding the psychology behind each person is important. Keep yourself up-to-date on new trends and attend workshops that teach you how to put them into action.

- **Reach a Breaking Point**

Hitting rock-bottom isn't always a bad thing. If you allow yourself to become broken, you are going to find that your leadership qualities improve. If you are in the position of leading right now, think back to what broke you. Did you have a moment in your life where you decided that you needed to be better? If so, consider that the experience drove you even further than you thought possible.

- **Embrace Opportunities**

Each time an obstacle is thrown into your path, embrace it as an opportunity to grow and learn. If you continually embrace the opportunities thrown your way, you are going to see your leadership grow, experiencing new skills and new ways of life. Each opportunity that is given to you is a chance for you to grow - or perhaps even change direction. Embrace these opportunities and go with the flow.

- **Be Focused on Your Vision**

You have a vision for your life. If you are a leader, you also need to have a vision for your team. Keep your focus on this vision and do not allow yourself to falter. With each opportunity, an obstacle that is thrown your way, look for a chance to grow, realigning your direction with your vision, and moving towards making that vision a reality.

- **Get Inspired**

Inspiration is a form of effective leadership. To be inspirational, you yourself first have to be inspired. Take some time to find what is inspirational, using that as a springboard to inspiring others. When you find yourself feeling less than effective, seek out inspiration to spark that fire and get you going again. Do not allow yourself to give up, because when you give up you are letting your team down.

- **Speak Up Often**

When you see injustice in the world, let your voice be heard; there's a good chance someone needs you. As a leader, you should focus not only on your own well-being but also on the well-being of others. This includes people in your community and those sharing the world with you. Make sure that when you disagree with something, speak up and let your opinion be heard. Others may be thinking the same thing but are afraid to say it out loud! You can be their voice.

- **Look at Potential, Not the Past**

In the workplace, it's important to look at the potential in individuals to determine if they have a spot on your team. If you let their past control your decision, you could be missing the opportunity to let someone shine. There are obvious reasons to look at their past (such as a criminal record), but often it's going to benefit you more to see the potential in a person rather than focusing on their past failures.

- **Recognize That You Are Good Enough**

When you recognize that you are good enough to be a leader, you are going to see better outcomes. There is no room in leadership for self-doubt or self-criticism. You need to give yourself the opportunity to embrace who you are and what you can accomplish. If you are down on yourself, you will not accomplish what you are setting out to. If you struggle with self-doubt, remember affirmations are a good way to shove that doubt out of the way.

- **Build on Your Strengths**

You listed your strengths already; build your leadership on those strengths. If you are an effective communicator, use that strength to communicate your vision. Perhaps you are good at negotiating, but your communication is less than stellar, build upon the negotiating qualities that you have to drive your team.

- **Be Courageous**

Leading requires courage. Courage comes from belief in yourself and your abilities. Do what you have to so that you can be courageous as you move forward into the future. Each obstacle that appears should be faced fearlessly. Do not worry about what could happen; just embrace the opportunity as it comes. When you do this, you are facing life full of courage.

- **Don't Look Past Yourself for Affirmation**

You do not need somebody else's approval to be effective. You are simply enough the way that you are. If you look for approval from someone else, you are going to be disappointed. The best place to get the approval that you need is by looking in the mirror and repeating the affirmations that we have discussed. Affirmations are vital to your success, and they need to come from within yourself.

- **Embrace the Spotlight**

As a leader, you are going to be in the spotlight regularly. When something good happens, you are going to be singled out – which always feels great. On the other hand, when something bad happens, you are going to be singled out – which is not always so great. Learn to embrace the focus that is going to be placed upon you because once you do that, you are going to find that you deal with the obstacles and the opportunities much more effectively.

- **You Know What You Stand For**

If you do not know what your values are, you are going to in life and in leadership. You need to stick by what you believe and stand up for the injustices that you see throughout the world. Standing firmly on your values is going to bring you far in life, and this is also going to give you the courage to face adversity. When you clearly define what it is you stand for, each obstacle that comes your way will have no effect on you. Instead, you are going to tackle each obstacle head-on.

Leadership can be scary, but when you practice and learn new skills, you find that your leadership is more effective, and you are gaining confidence in this role. Understanding what your superpower is, what type of leader you are, and how these work together is going to keep you on a straight path to success.

Conclusion

Thank you for making it through to the end of Mindset. You are on your way to unlocking the power of positive thinking and skyrocketing your confidence, success, self-discipline, productivity, focus, self-esteem, mental toughness, social intelligence, and leadership skills. It has been a joy writing this book; I hope it was informative, providing you with all the tools you need to achieve your goals - whatever they may be.

The next step is to work on positive thinking:

- Take responsibility for your present and your future
- Learn and practice living each day with joy
- Practice self-compassion and learn to control your thoughts
- Be in control of your own life and boost your confidence
- Understand who you are and accept responsibility for that person
- Decide what you want your future to look like
- Begin living life on your own terms
- Set goals for yourself
- Learn to face your fears and take action
- Readjust your thought processes
- View obstacles as opportunities

- Commit to improving yourself in your relationships
- Focus on meditation and improving your concentration
- Make a commitment to beat procrastination and become more productive
- Learn how to use affirmations positively in your life
- Understand the concept of mental toughness and how to practice this skill
- Work to improve your social intelligence as well as your social skills
- Understand how your leadership affects those around you as well are your own destiny.

Finally, if you found this book useful in any way, a review on Amazon is always appreciated! Good luck on the journey ahead; I wish you much success in life.

www.ingramcontent.com/pod-product-compliance
Lightning Source LLC
Chambersburg PA
CBHW070049230426
43661CB00005B/823